Praise for *Navigating Emotional Realities with Adults*

"A foundational tool for leadership development."
–Sharon Jackson, Program Director,
Omaha Bridges Out of Poverty, Nebraska

"Never before have public education and the workforce shared a crisis like we share today. The ability to create safe and supportive learning and work environments will make the difference in recruiting and retaining great employees. This learning about our 'emotional brain' is a key part of the answer."
–Vern Reed, Former Director of Under-Resourced
Student Services, Ottumwa Schools, Iowa

*"*Navigating Emotional Realities with Adults *brings all the data, research, and education we know and value in* Emotional Poverty in All Demographics *and* Emotional Poverty, Volume 2 *to work with us. This book took me on a journey backward through my childhood and then to where I hope my future lies. Our workplaces do not have to be places we dread; in fact, the information brought to us in this book can transform workplaces into places we value and thrive in. I encourage you to first read this book and then share with your coworkers, friends, and family."*
–Loran Mayes, Professional Development Coordinator,
Eastern Oklahoma State College GEAR UP

"Businesses are facing unprecedented challenges in today's marketplace including labor shortages, high turnover, low employee engagement, and increasing workplace violence. This material gives insight into the science of human emotions and adult development that business leaders can utilize to improve employee morale, which in turn improves overall business performance."
–Kristy Gebhart, Regional Vice President,
Partners Personnel, Indianapolis, Indiana

NAVIGATING
EMOTIONAL
realities
WITH ADULTS

Emotional Poverty at Work

Ruby K. Payne, Ph.D. and Jim Ott, S.Psy.S.
Navigating Emotional Realities with Adults: Emotional Poverty at Work
160 pages
Bibliography: pages 129–133

ISBN: 978-1-948244-55-8

aha! Process, Inc.
P.O. Box 727
Highlands, TX 77562-0727
(800) 424-9484 ▪ (281) 426-5300
Fax: (281) 426-5600
ahaprocess.com

Book design by Paula Nicolella
Cover design by Amy Alick Perich

Printed in White Plains, Maryland

Library of Congress Control Number: 2022921851

NAVIGATING
EMOTIONAL
realities
WITH ADULTS

Emotional Poverty at Work

Ruby K. Payne, Ph.D.
and Jim Ott, S.Psy.S.

Table of Contents

Acknowledgments

The authors are grateful for the long-term input of aha! Process national consultants and all the individuals across the world who use the work and give us invaluable feedback about our Framework, Bridges, and Emotional Poverty work. We are especially indebted to Rubén Perez for allowing us to use his story "A Hole in Your Heart" as an interlude in this book. We also want to acknowledge the support staff at aha! Process, especially Jesse Conrad, Peg Conrad, and Paula Nicolella, who were instrumental in getting this book finished and published.

Ruby Payne: I wish to acknowledge my husband, Tee Bowman, who knows and supports the amount of bandwidth writing a book takes. I deeply appreciate the patience of everyone throughout all the renditions, changes, deletions, and additions. I am particularly grateful for Peg Conrad and the myriad ways in which she works with all the players to get the book finished.

Jim Ott: I would like to acknowledge with gratitude the partnership and wisdom of three aha! Process consultants who were important in the development of this work: Ermina Soler, Vern Reed, and Daisy Mastroianni. I would also like to acknowledge the staff, parents, and students of the Bellevue Community School District in Iowa, especially Superintendent Tom Meyer, Principal Jeff Recker, and Alternative Education Teacher Rick Casel, whose support and encouragement allowed the freedom to explore many of these topics through classroom and small group discussions. Finally, I am grateful for the support and encouragement of my wife, Teresa, during this project.

Introduction

Emotional poverty in the workplace: You probably see a lot of it. Not only in others but in yourself. You may ask yourself, "Why did I do that? What was that about? Why am I unhappy at work? What makes me love this job? Why do my coworkers irritate me so much?" You might think, "That boss—such a jerk," or, "I love my boss!" What makes this happen?

The world of work is by nature stressful. There are so many deadlines to meet, goals to achieve, and personality differences to contend with. The authors' hope in writing *Navigating Emotional Realities with Adults* is to ease the tension adults experience in the workplace and help them achieve well-being outside of work, on their own time. When we better understand the stress, we can reduce it through the application of informed strategies.

This book, which includes portions of Ruby Payne's *Emotional Poverty in All Demographics* and *Emotional Poverty, Volume 2*, is intended for use by organizations to address adult interactions in the workplace, and it includes sections that guide individuals in considering their own emotional experiences.

The purpose of this book is to help you negotiate the emotional realities of your workplace, as well as your emotional responses to the workplace. There are *tons* of books on leadership and getting promoted, but how do you navigate the workplace emotionally? Often, it is about dealing with difficult people, personality styles, manipulation, and persuasion.

I, Ruby, always want to continue growing and learning. For many years, I have had mentors, coaches, therapists, and advisors with many different areas of expertise. Working with these experts and drawing on research findings from neuroscience, quantum biology, epigenetics, and clinical psychology, I have been trying to answer questions like these: How do our emotions develop? What happens in the environment to impact our emotional development as we relate to people? And what are the emotional patterns from our families that we replicate in the workplace?

This book is basically Emotions 101. It is for laypeople, but it is not meant to replace therapy or a therapist. It will not answer all the questions you may have about issues in your own life, and it will not equip you to practice therapy on others. It is simply meant to provide a basic understanding of the brain, the emotional self, relationships, and emotional issues in the workplace.

Neurobiology model[1]

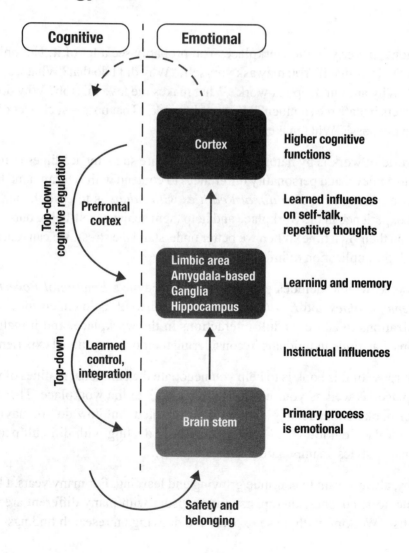

In the model of the neurobiological system, the primary process is emotional. The self-reflection, memory associations, and higher-order thinking required by the workplace all occur after people feel their feelings. One aim of this book is to help employers understand the workplace dynamics that keep employees from achieving.

When employers focus only on the cognitive interventions and understandings listed on the left-hand side of the neurobiology model, this limits the ability of the entire workplace to address emotional realities. Until there is a general understanding of the emotional structures in the brain, their full or partial development, and their impact on the workplace in terms of productivity, retention, and well-being, the ability of the workplace to tap the full potential of its employees is limited. This book focuses on understanding the right-hand side of this chart and fully developing those brain structures we use to negotiate our emotional realities.

Here are some basics in the science about emotions:

1. All emotional wellness is based in safety and belonging.

2. It is difficult to change behavior. It is much easier to change the motivation for the behavior, which then changes the behavior.

3. The biggest difference between healthy (beneficial) and unhealthy (unbeneficial) behavior is compassion—for yourself and others.

4. Workplaces will always have consequences. It is the approach to emotional realities that needs to change.

5. The amygdala is mostly structured by the time you are three years old. It is restructured in adolescence.

6. At their base level, emotions are simple—you are either moving toward something or away from something. That is why it is not possible for the brain to be both angry and compassionate at the same time. Anger is an "away from" emotion that often results in attack. Compassion is a "moving toward" emotion that usually results in understanding.

7. To change a behavior or response, the behavior or response has to be named.

Please note: This approach does not see a difficult person as "bad" or "sick" but rather as someone who is injured. We look at how to approach a person so that everyone—both individuals and organizations—can function at a higher level of safety and belonging.

'Once upon a time'

"Once upon a time" is the opening of a story structure with which we are all familiar. So much so that as soon as we hear the opening, "Once upon a time…," we hear the ending line in our minds: "They all lived happily ever after." If only it were so easy! In the childhood fairy tales we are familiar with, "once upon a time" sets the stage. It is a description of the problem that will require some type of intervention in order to result in a "happily ever after" resolution. In fairy tales, that intervention is usually magical.

Fairy tales were not always this way. A quick search reveals the original versions of the stories on which our versions of fairy tales are based, and they don't always end well. Before Sleeping Beauty awoke, there were many princes who tried to get to her but died, impaled on thorns. The evil queen in the original Snow White story meets a much worse fate than she does in the Disney movie version. Hans Christian Andersen's Little Mermaid does not marry the human prince. The original versions of fairy tales are dark—and maybe truer to real life than the sanitized movie versions we have come to know.

Life is hard. Magic is rare. "Happily ever afters" don't happen just because we want them to. It takes time, effort, and intentionality to deal with our "once upon a times." And we all have a "once upon a time": a setting for the life story into which we were born.

Navigating Emotional Realities with Adults is about understanding both others' and our own "once upon a time" stories. It is about using what we know about child and adult development, as well as neurology and brain science, to understand others' stories, our own stories, and how our stories intersect with our coworkers and the people we serve in our work. It's also a book about working toward the "happily ever after" we all hope to experience. "Happily ever after" not only in life, but at the end of each day and at the end of each encounter we have with others.

Everyone has a "once upon a time…" From the moment we are born—indeed, even before we are born—we are in a story based on the characters and experiences we will encounter in the context into which we are born. Our story begins before we are old enough to tell it to anyone, including ourselves. As we grow and develop language, we participate in our story through interaction and communication with others and through thinking and talking to ourselves about what we are experiencing. And then: puberty! Everything—from your best friends to your basal ganglia—gets amplified, reshuffled, realigned, and refined.

Moving from adolescence to adulthood, we take with us a story that was partially written for us and that we have partially written for ourselves. That story becomes the foundation of who we think we are, how we think the world works, and how we best navigate life with a sense of purpose and control. It informs how we interact with others in our lives, including family, friends, coworkers, and those we meet more casually, like employees of businesses and restaurants we frequent. Every interaction takes place in the context of the story we are telling ourselves. These interactions include self-talk, or the internal dialogue we have with ourselves as we work to make sense of the world and the challenges we face. This story develops throughout our lives, but it all begins at birth. In many ways, adulthood is our interpretation and application of what we learned as children.

While there are many characters in our individual stories, there is one character that is a part of every person's story. This character, in many ways, functions as the villain in all of our stories. It presents itself as a sometimes quiet, sometimes loud voice in our heads. Sometimes it is not a voice at all but a deep-seated feeling; we feel it in our gut, as we like to say. This feeling opposes us and works to tear us down and separate us from others. It functions like the magic spell in a fairy tale and traps us.

This character is shame. Once it has us trapped, we want to be rescued, but we are afraid of what our rescuer will think of us if they actually see us. Shame has received a lot of attention in recent times. That's a good thing because shame loses much of its power when it is brought out into the open. But all the attention that shame has received has not made it disappear for any of us. Being aware of the influence of shame in our adult relationships is important. When we recognize shame's influence on our sense of self and on the health of the relationships that matter most, we can mediate its influence on both. Dealing with shame works best in transparent, mutually respectful relationships situated in a broader community that is able to address conflicts and tensions in a healthy way.

Dealing with emotional realities in healthy ways increases emotional intelligence. One of the seminal works on emotional intelligence is Daniel Goleman's book *Emotional Intelligence: Why It Can Matter More Than IQ*. Since 1995, when that book was first published, the interest in emotional functioning and mental health has grown by leaps and bounds. One reason for this interest is the expansion of scientific knowledge about how the brain processes emotions. Alongside the increase in knowledge, we have seen growing levels of stress partially due to the increase in access to information and stories available at the touch of a button. In the rural United States in the 1800s, regular access to information was limited to newspapers, books, and the local gossip mill. Today, we have access to billions of stories in every format imaginable. We no longer worry about the stories and opinions of just the people down the lane; we can now consider millions of people whose stories include war, poverty, oppression, hunger, and human trafficking.

Our emotional resources are being taxed in ways that did not exist before the 1990s, when the Internet took its place as the primary force shaping the world. All of us know that when we are stressed and low on emotional resources, we tend to have less control of our emotional reactions. In the same way our intellectual resources are burdened by a complex calculus problem, our emotional resources are strained by the flood of emotional information and experiences that characterizes our media-saturated world. In the book *Bridges Out of Poverty*, the authors talk about being trapped in "the tyranny of the moment," a space in which the demands of the environment overwhelm the available resources. Many contemporary cultures also seem to be trapped in an emotional tyranny of the moment. As people search for understanding and relief, interest in mental health issues increases. Ruby Payne's books *Emotional Poverty* and *Emotional Poverty, Volume 2* address emotional well-being primarily for students, teachers, and other people working in schools. *Navigating Emotional Realities with Adults* widens the lens to help adults in every context better understand our stories and the stories of others.

Emotional intelligence: Understanding both our own and others' emotions and using that knowledge to make things better for everyone.

I, Jim, developed this definition of emotional intelligence over the course of a school year by considering the issue with high school focus groups. The resulting definition was one the high school students understood and could embrace. On its face it seems very simple, but it is hard to put into practice. Nevertheless, using emotional understanding to maximize outcomes for everyone is an essential part of building "happily ever after" stories at home, at work, and in the community.

The majority of this book examines stages and processes that impact the development of our stories. We consider our personal development from birth through adolescence and recognize how the story we end up with as adults is a continuation of the story we learned about ourselves as we grew up. The adult version of ourself is our interpretation and application of our childhood experiences, but we also recognize that our development doesn't stop when we become adults. At each stage of life, we have opportunities to consider and amend our stories so that they better match who we are and what we hope for in life—our "happily ever after."

The end of each section of the book is designed for those who want to go deeper into the material through personal application. There are also suggestions for team activities and approaches to better understanding ourselves, our coworkers, and our clients and customers.

The concepts in this book are for all adults, especially those who are interested in improving their workplace climate and reducing stress and frustration.

The principles of understanding ourselves and others apply whether you are a schoolteacher or a business owner, a healthcare provider or a social worker, a police officer or a pastor. We are all in the midst of our own stories, interacting with the stories of others, and hoping to write a grander story that includes our families and communities as well. We all have a "once upon a time." Together we can build a future story that brings about more "happily ever afters" for ourselves and the people around us.

Everyone has a 'once upon a time'

Once upon a time, a baby was born. The baby was different from every other baby, but like every other baby, this baby had characteristics and inclinations passed on from the baby's parents. The baby had no control over those characteristics and inclinations.

The baby had the same needs as any other baby. The baby needed a parent or parents who loved that child perfectly—love expressed by modeling healthy adult relationships and emotional regulation, which would create a sense of safety for the baby. The baby needed to be attended to by parents who were not so attentive that they inhibited the baby's natural need to explore and grow. The baby needed to experience love expressed in firmly enforced boundaries, but within those boundaries there should be nothing but unconditional love and delight. The baby needed the love expressed by caregivers who understood that this baby was unique and not like other babies, even the ones in the same family.

However, who among us gets all this? No one gets the kind of love idealized in the paragraphs above. Most of us get the best our parent or parents can give, and as children we have little to no control over the ways in which our parents' love differs from the ideal. However, we are not here to blame our parents. This is not a criticism of parents but a recognition that no matter how much parents love their children, there will always be openings for insecurities to develop, and these insecurities impact our neurological development. The fact is that the vast majority of parents are doing the best they can with what they have and what they know. And there are many contexts into which children are born and in which they are raised. There are two-parent families and single parents, nuclear families and multigenerational families, children raised by biological parents and children raised by adoptive parents, children raised by stepparents and children raised by grandparents. All of these parents do the best they can to guide, protect, and encourage their children. But even when caregivers have the best of intentions, the combinations of the adults' own backgrounds and the children's unique characteristics and needs result in a "once upon a time" backstory for every child, a backstory that includes unmet needs. From the earliest moments, a baby's brain is working to figure out how the world works and who the self and others are. Babies do this in light of their needs, the extent to which their needs are fulfilled, and the emotional insecurities experienced because of the needs that go unfulfilled.

The baby's brain is storing these emotional memories in the feeling part of the brain, the limbic system and brain stem. The memories are not verbal or language-based. The part of the brain that processes experiences in language doesn't really get going until the age of three or four. You can check this out right now. Tell a story about something that happened when you were one or two years old. Most people can't. Some can remember moments, usually accompanied by a strong feeling, but we can't tell complete narrative stories about those events because our brains weren't able to hold memories that way when we were that age.

We may not have narrative stories from before age three, but we had all experienced plenty of feelings by the time we were three. Anyone who has been around children from infancy until age three knows that emotional expression is not lacking in this age group! And because no one's upbringing was perfect, we experienced many distressing emotions, including anger, sadness, fear, and anxiety. Perhaps even worse, neurological science is discovering that children as young as 18 months are experiencing what can be recognized as shame. The villain in the story is making trouble before it even has a voice. Shame is already speaking with a deep emotion that conveys its message physically. That pit you sometimes feel in your stomach, for example, communicates feelings of "less than" and "separate from"; feelings of shame tell babies they lack value and that the environment and the people in it can't be trusted.

By the time we are three years old, much of the limbic system in the brain is structurally developed. Changes can and will happen, especially during adolescence, but the foundation of how we will deal with emotions, including the voice of shame, is laid before we have language to identify and understand those emotions. Some of those emotional reactions lead to deep insecurities about ourselves, the world, and others. In many ways, we spend the rest of our lives working to address the insecurities and shame that result from our earliest experiences.

Once upon a time in 'the real world'

Once upon a time, there was a little boy who had been a baby but was a baby no longer. That little person grew and became a teenager on his way to becoming a young adult. And the older he got, the more people he had to deal with. What started as a relational world in which the baby interacted with only a few caregivers and siblings had become a world in which the boy had to navigate relationships at school, on the baseball team, in the neighborhood, at church—everywhere he went, more and more relationships! The most important relationships were those with his family, but the boy he had become through his family was discovering who he was in the context of others. The identity he had developed at home was being tested in "the real world."

At the center of all of our stories is our sense of who we are. Our early years are spent constructing a self. We form an internal image of ourselves based on information we receive from outside ourselves. No one exists in a vacuum, and we only know who we are in the context of our relationships with others. As we move through our single-digit years, our brains begin to store autobiographical memories in the hippocampus, and those deep memories become the material we use to construct our sense of self. One of our goals during this stage of development is to address distressing emotions through various strategies and behaviors aimed at getting needs met and avoiding emotional pain. During this period of our childhood, we are learning to navigate the world of relationships and trying to control our experiences by making choices that will bring about the results we desire.

Very little of this calculation and navigation is conscious, of course. But the brain is constantly asking questions to determine solutions to the problems of being safe and having a sense of belonging—questions like:

- What happens when I laugh? What happens when I hide? What happens when I yell, cry, etc.?

- How can I get the attention of my caregiver? Or in some situations, how can I avoid their attention?

- What makes me feel safe?

- What can I do when I am worried?

- What do I have to do to get my siblings to leave me alone?

The questions are endless, and a kid has plenty of insecurities, including a sense of shame, by the time the kid is three years old. Nobody, child or adult, likes to feel insecurity brought on by sadness, anger, anxiety, or shame, but everyone experiences these emotions in their formative years. The people we become and the personalities we develop are partially an attempt to mediate or even avoid those uncomfortable feelings.

Our sense of self is strongly influenced by shame. We are constantly deciding what we can show on the outside that will gain us the affirmation of our families, schools, workplaces, and communities. At the same time, we are making decisions about what to keep hidden. Shame eventually leads to negative self-talk: "There is something wrong with me that is not wrong with everyone else, and I can't let anyone know or they will reject me."

Much of what we are attempting to do and be in the world is about maintaining a sense of control over our circumstances. This includes wanting relationships that are predictable and stable. When relationships are unstable in our childhood, we try to amend our behavior in ways that restore equilibrium. When our attempts to maintain control over our circumstances are unsuccessful, we internalize the "failure" as a personal fault. It might not make sense to an adult, but small children see themselves at the center of the universe. To a small child, everything that happens is related to that child because that's how a child's mind works. If an attempt to control circumstances fails, even partially, the child thinks, "I must have done something wrong, or I must be something wrong; otherwise, this wouldn't have happened to me." This is why kids who are in their single-digit years when their parents divorce or separate often believe they must have caused their parents to divorce—that it is somehow their fault. They believe this in spite of all the messages from parents, relatives, teachers, and counselors telling them the opposite: "Mommy and Daddy may not love each other anymore, but they both love you just as much as they ever did." There is a reason parents splitting up is one of the 10 adverse childhood experiences (ACEs). We have spoken to many teenagers who know that their parents' divorce was not their fault, but it *feels* like it was.

Based on our childhood experiences, we develop strategies to try to control our circumstances and the people around us. These strategies are somewhat, but never fully, successful. Because they are unsuccessful, the voice of shame continues to attack our sense of our value in the world. With the advent of adolescence, shame is partnered with an increased ability to think abstractly and engage in metacognition—to think about our thinking. Our powers of perspective-taking increase. We are better able to think about what others might be thinking of us. And shame always tells us that others are thinking bad things about us or that they *would* think bad things about us if they knew what we were really like inside. This is a common experience for many people during the emotionally charged period of adolescence.

Through adolescence, we mature physically, experience new levels and nuances of emotion, and engage in relationships of ever-increasing complexity. The brain undergoes rewiring in response to the increase in stress and the new kinds of problem solving required. But often, the strategies we developed to navigate our childhood world continue to be our go-to options in dealing with this new, not-quite-adult world. Parents of teenagers say things like, "He was just as stubborn when he was eight as he is now!" or, "She was always an easygoing child."

Unfortunately, our childhood strategies, which were at least marginally successful when we were young, are increasingly less effective in meeting the demands of adolescence and adult life. This is a period during which some people self-medicate in an attempt to mediate the stress and insecurities of life. Self-medication can come in many forms, including the obvious (food, sex, alcohol and other drugs, video games, social media), but also tendencies toward rigid self-control: Perfectionism is an example. Control is also a category in which self-harm, eating disorders, and suicide reside. Self-medication brings immediate relief to uncomfortable emotions but does nothing to resolve the underlying causes of those emotions. When the feelings return to the conscious mind, the person will often return just as quickly to the self-medication of choice.

This process can lead to addiction, and that further entrenches a cycle in which the voice of shame plays a major role.

The cycle goes something like this:

- Life is stressful. We all go through periods of stress. Prolonged, chronic stress can be overwhelming.

- Because stress taxes our system physically, mentally, and emotionally, we desire escape. We want a break. The voice of shame can enter the conversation subtly with the message: "You deserve some relief." The voice of shame is most easily recognized as one that promotes self-entitlement ("You deserve more!"), but also self-condemnation ("How could you?").

- Immediate relief is often available. Looking for relief is a kind of self-medication. Sometimes it is healthy relief—take a walk, talk with someone, distract with a book or even a television show. But some forms of relief can lead to dependence. Relief is the goal, not addiction. Once we start to look to our self-medication of choice, we can get trapped in the need. Obvious examples of self-medication that can go awry include pornography, drugs, alcohol, food, anger, social media, and video games. It can start slowly. The self-entitlement voice of shame says, "It's just this once, and besides, after everything you have been through…" We learn to justify the choices we make that can lead to dependence and addiction.

- The self-condemning voice of shame strikes an accusatory tone with thoughts like, "What is wrong with you? You should be stronger than this and be able to handle life better. What would people think if they knew?"

- As dependence on self-medication takes firm hold of our lives, the voice of shame may be reinforced by condemnation from people in our lives who recognize the problem but aren't supportive.

- The combination of internal and external shaming voices can lead to a sense of inadequacy and lack of confidence in our ability to meet the stresses of life.

- This adds to the chronic stress we are experiencing, which can take us back to the top of the list: "Life is stressful. We all go through periods of stress. Prolonged, chronic stress can be overwhelming…"

- Many of us continue to experience the cycle until we get help.

Perhaps you recognize some version of this process in yourself or someone you care about.

We all have cycles like this as a part of our neurological makeup and identity. The key is to recognize the cycle and interrupt it. In some cases, just being conscious of the cycle will allow a person to break the cycle and develop healthier responses to stress. In other situations, support may be needed through friends, counselors, and support groups like Alcoholics Anonymous. But in all cases, the cycle can be broken. The human brain is incredibly flexible; this flexibility is called neuroplasticity. It takes work and intention, but we can all learn new ways to process stress and the resulting emotions in ways that are healthy for ourselves and the people we care about.

As we come to the end of adolescence and head into our adult lives, we often think that we are leaving our childhood story behind. The reality is that our childhood story becomes the foundation on which we build our adult lives. Recall that our lives as adults are our interpretation and application of what we learned as children. Left unexamined, the strategies we developed in childhood continue to affect our adult relationships at home and at work. Often, the strategies that helped us when we were young become obstacles to establishing an adult version of ourselves that is informed by our past but not defined by it. We all know adults who act like children in certain situations. And we all know that we ourselves have moments when the little kid in us comes out.

The good news is that our childhood strategies can become our greatest strengths if we no longer use them to protect ourselves. For example, a child who learned to be perfect in order to gain some measure of control and affirmation will have developed a high level of performance and attention to detail that will be a powerful asset in many professions. The child who learned to be helpful and attentive to the needs of others to keep from being seen as needy will have the ability to help and support many people. In both of these cases, and in many others, the strategy for self-protection will be most effective if it is decoupled from the identity of the child the adult is still trying to protect.

A quick word about trauma: Everything we have considered is true for people who have experienced specific or complex trauma in their childhoods. However, trauma requires a more complex process for healing and rewiring the brain in order to escape the control of traumatic memories. Professional help will likely be required, but the ever-growing knowledge about how the brain processes trauma and how flexible the brain is in developing new patterns of thought provides hope for those who have experienced trauma in their pasts.

Throughout our early years, people ask us what we want to be when we grow up. Then, suddenly for some of us, we find we have grown up, and we ask ourselves, "Is this really what I want to be? Is this really who I want to be?"

Once upon a time in early adulthood

Once upon a time there was a little girl who grew up and emerged from adolescence as a young woman. It was time for her to leave home, and she set off into the world to find her own way. She took with her all the stories of her youth, including happy memories and some that were more challenging. She also took with her an understanding of relationships that was informed first by her family and then by those she met at school and in her first jobs. Now, as a young adult with her future ahead of her, she was finally independent and ready to start living independently. She was ready to work and live alongside other young adults with adult responsibilities, relationships, jobs, and bills. She had a lot of thoughts about what it means to be an adult, although at this point she had only experienced life as a child.

The young woman in the story is beginning a new journey. On this journey, it is possible to leave childish ways behind, but many people never do. As we enter adulthood, we are taking with us all the things we learned while we were growing up. These include strategies for handling money, solving problems, resolving conflict, defining roles and responsibilities, discovering what we believe about ourselves, coping with stress and anxiety, and many other strategies we learned as young people. The experience of growing up leaves us with a way of being in the world that makes sense to us. The problem is that when the strategies that worked for us as children are applied to adult situations and dilemmas, they don't always work so well.

As we live our adult stories, the voice of shame always works to anchor our sense of self to messages from our past—failures, embarrassing moments, incidents of pain and even abuse for which shame tells us we are responsible. The subtle message of shame is: "No one can know about this or about you, and you must continue to use the same self-protective strategies you have always used so no one ever finds out."

The idea that shame motivates self-protective strategies we developed in childhood is useful not only in understanding our own shame but also in understanding the actions and emotions of others. Because our brains are hypervigilant in keeping us safe and maintaining the stability and predictability of life, it is human nature for us to react negatively to people who exhibit behaviors that do not make sense to us. Our survival brain and our feeling brain combine to send an alert message: This person may pose a threat. When our thinking brain gets involved, it often tries to justify the emotional reaction we are having by being judgmental of the other person's character, intelligence, etc. Unless we are aware of this tendency in ourselves and actively work against it, we tend to resolve challenging interactions with others through the lens of judgment. This results in divisions that inhibit the establishment of relationships of mutual respect, which are necessary if we are to be our best and do our best work. Because guess what? That other person is judging you just as much as you are judging them, and you both think your perspective makes sense. The reality is that you are both making sense of emotional reactions that happen when there is a lack of understanding of each other.

The emotional reactions and actions of others that are the most troubling for us are usually a manifestation of a self-protective strategy developed in childhood and/or after experiencing trauma. When we can look at other people through a lens of curiosity and compassion instead of judgment, we are more effective in our jobs, our relationships, and our lives generally. And we will be more content with ourselves.

We have been considering our "once upon a time" stories with an eye toward living a story with a "happily ever after" ending. Nobody is out there trying to live a "happily never after" story! As we have discovered, our stories are very complicated, with parts being written when we are very young, before we have the ability to consider the impact our stories have on who we are. We have no control over the life into which we were born, but as we get older, we learn to cope as effectively as possible, and we begin trying very hard to control our circumstances. Without self-awareness and intentional work, we can end up trying to navigate the adult world and solve adult problems using childhood strategies. And all the time, the voice of shame is accusing us, belittling us, and assuring us that shame's strategy of hiding and self-protection is the best one.

The good news is that there is a lot of information out there about emotions, neurological development, and strategies for dealing with how our brains work—information that wasn't known 50 or even 25 years ago. There are strategies that can help us sort out our brains and get them moving in the direction we wish. It's all about learning to use our minds to develop self-control—to have an integrated brain and regulate our emotional reactions. We can stop using personality and emotion to try to control circumstances and other people. The goal is not to eliminate emotions. Emotions are useful and necessary. The goal is to understand what our emotions and physical bodies are communicating to us. Then we can use an integrated brain to regulate the thoughts and actions that accompany the emotions.

What follows are some ideas and suggestions that may be useful for you in your own work to better understand yourself and the people you live and work with. There has never been a time when people were under more stress globally, and there has never been a time when developing stronger emotional intelligence was more necessary or more valuable. Recall the definition from earlier:

Emotional intelligence: Understanding both our own and others' emotions and using that understanding to make things better for everyone.

As we become more emotionally intelligent by integrating and regulating our brains, we better understand and address our own insecurities while helping others do the same. We will be better employees, partners, parents, community members, and teammates. We will become a part of writing "happily ever after" stories for ourselves, our friends, our families, and those we know and work with.

Here's to your "happily ever after!"

Personal and group application

Included in each chapter of the book are activities and questions for further exploration. Here we include additional ways you and the staff in your organization or business can explore some of these issues in more depth. For each section of the book, we will include:

- Journaling questions and prompts

- Discussion questions for staff

- Activities to explore

Journaling is a powerful tool for introspection. Many people who regularly write in a journal report that they sometimes surprise themselves with what they write. It's almost as if the brain "runs into content" it didn't know it was going to find. Writing engages many parts of the brain: fine and gross motor skills, letter formation or typing dexterity, spelling, sentence construction, and so on. If you haven't tried journaling, this might be the time give it a try.

The staff discussion questions are designed to keep the conversation going. Everything we do at work occurs in the context of relationships. When we are intentional about having conversations about our social and emotional lives, we can head conflict off at the pass and be more effective in working together for the people our organization serves.

The activities to explore can be carried out on your own or in a group. They are aimed at helping you cultivate a more fully integrated and regulated brain.

Journaling questions and prompts

- What are three emotional challenges you face as a part of your work? Write about these challenges as the beginning of a "work journal" as you look forward to applying the information in this book.

- Write an emotional goal or two based on a survey of the book's content or what you have learned up this point. For example:

  - "I will work to be less frustrated with _____." (This could be a person, a process, or even yourself.)

  - "In six months, I will reduce my stress level at work by applying the concepts in this book."

- Make your goals as specific as possible so you can measure your progress.

Discussion questions for staff

- What "cognitive interventions" (rules and regulations, procedures, etc.) are present in this workplace that contribute to emotional stress? Are any of them able to be modified?

- Use the list of basics to open a discussion on this topic. Is this new information? Which of these basics would it be good for us to learn more about?

Activities to explore

Box it up

As you are beginning this journey, consider writing down your workplace stress issues on index cards and putting them in a box at the beginning of the workday. Practice telling yourself that you are going to leave them in the box until the end of the day rather than letting them control your thinking during the day. Any kind of "box" will do. A tissue box, an envelope, a drawer—you could even write them down and leave them in the car if you drive to work.

Chapter One

Safety and Belonging

All emotional wellness is based in two things: safety and belonging. Whenever we get upset, intuitively we believe that our safety or belonging is jeopardized in some manner.

A little quiz – Do you feel safe at work?

Place a check mark next to the items that are true about your workplace.

1. I have a person at work I can talk to about my performance without fear of reprisal.

2. If I tell my supervisor something confidentially, it stays confidential.

3. My supervisor is consistent and predictable.

4. When my work is examined and criticized, it is not about me personally.

5. Work goals are given in advance. Support to meet those goals is available.

6. I trust my boss/supervisor—even if I don't like them. I know they will do what they say they will do.

7. Workplace ethics—integrity, legality, and honesty—are part of the company culture.

8. Unscrupulous behavior and unwanted advances are dealt with immediately.

9. Differences and diversity are accepted. The focus is on the value I bring to the workplace.

10. I am blamed for things I have no control over.

11. Clients/customers scream and yell at me.

12. I have little control over my work hours.

13. I never know when my boss/supervisor will lose their temper.

A little quiz – Do you feel like you belong?

Place a check mark next to the items that are true about your workplace.

1. I am included in meetings that are important to my work assignments.

2. In team meetings, my ideas are entertained and discussed.

3. I am included in work lunches.

4. I have colleagues at work with whom I socialize outside of work.

5. There is a businesslike, focused energy at work, and people tend to work together for a common purpose.

6. I agree with the values of the company I work for.

To better understand how all this develops, let's take a look at our autonomic nervous system and basic brain development.

The autonomic nervous system

Every human being has an autonomic nervous system, and it controls about 99.9% of your reactions. It has two subsystems—the SNS (sympathetic nervous system) and the PNS (parasympathetic nervous system). The SNS is the "fire alarm"—it tells you: "You are in trouble, and you better do something about it!" The PNS is the "calm down, calm down" system.

Your body is basically an energy system. Everything that happens in your body is either a chemical or electrical interaction. Your body is an electromagnetic system. If you have ever been in a room with an angry person, you can feel their anger. Waves from your heart go three feet out from your body. The waves from the heart have 60 times the amplitude of brain waves.

Autonomic nervous system (ANS) mental model

- Everything that happens in your body is a chemical/electrical interaction

- Your body is an energy system

ANS has two subsystems

(gas pedal)   (brakes)

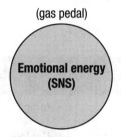   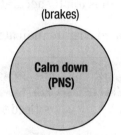

SNS (sympathetic nervous system)
- Fight/flight
- Intense joy/creativity
- Sensitive/reactive to trauma
- Hijacks the amygdala under stress
- Immune system stops functioning
- Digestive system stops
- Heart rate increases
- Fire alarm

PNS (parasympathetic nervous system)
- Rest and digest
- Calm down
- Body can heal

These two systems are integrated and regulated by the prefrontal cortex

(clutch)

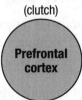

Safety and belonging

Your autonomic nervous system (ANS) immediately reacts if you think your safety or belonging is jeopardized. The SNS goes off, signaling you are in danger. Immediately, your PNS attempts to calm you down. In the process, your body gives "body tells" as your system tries to address the issue.

Emotions are processed much faster than thought (200–5,000 times faster) because emotions are energy. Joe Navarro was an FBI agent for many years, and in his book, *What Every Body Is Saying*, he identifies a discomfort-detecting and pacifying approach to understanding emotional responses. Body tells indicate the level of comfort/discomfort the individual is experiencing. Navarro used this system to help law enforcement officials identify the truth in many cases. However, he is very careful to say that there is no one way to identify the truth and that no system is totally accurate.

Here is a simplified chart to indicate some of the body tells:

Freeze (first response)	Flight (next response)	Fight (last response)
▪ Stop movement	▪ Need to get away	▪ Attack
▪ Hold breath or breathe from the chest	▪ Turn away from the person	▪ Not look at you
▪ Restrict motion	▪ Evade conversation	▪ Verbal assault
▪ Try to be invisible	▪ Close or rub the eyes	▪ Sarcasm, denigration
▪ If abused, may avoid contact; arms will go dormant trying not to be seen	▪ Cover face with hands	▪ Lean forward toward you
	▪ Lean away	▪ Torso will begin moving
	▪ Turn feet toward exit	
	▪ Distance oneself	

What is a pacifying behavior?

A pacifying behavior is a behavior that is meant to soothe yourself. Look for the pattern of discomfort followed by a soothing behavior. Pacifying behaviors help signal what things trouble or distress a person.

A pattern that often occurs is that the individual will signal discomfort—e.g., leaning away, frowning, crossing or tensing arms. This signaling of discomfort is often followed by a pacifying behavior. The brain requires the body to do something that will stimulate nerve endings, which releases calming endorphins in the brain so that the limbic system can be soothed.

Examples of pacifying behaviors

- Neck touching or stroking; touching the suprasternal notch (the indented area below the Adam's apple and the breastbone—sometimes referred to as the neck dimple); the neck has a lot of nerve endings and, when stroked, lowers blood pressure and heart rate

- Massaging/stroking the face, playing with hair

- Exhaling slowly with puffed cheeks

- Using the tongue inside the mouth to massage cheeks or lips

- If chewing gum, will chew faster

- Touching head, face, neck, shoulder, arm

- Men may stroke face or beard, adjust ties

- Women may touch necks, clothes, jewelry, hair

- Tapping a pencil or drumming fingers

- Playing with objects—pens, lipstick, etc.

- Excessive yawning

- Leg cleansing—moving your hands up and down your legs

Note: The information that follows is about patterns. These patterns must be considered in context, and it is important to note the changes a person makes in the course of a conversation. It is the changes that are important to watch, particularly if they differ from that person's nonverbal tendencies. No one indicator is the whole picture. You must observe the patterns and combinations.

Body part	Comfortable	Uncomfortable
Legs/feet	- Staying where they are - Moving towards you	- Turning away from you - Moving away from you - Wrapping legs around chair legs - Kicking up with foot

(continued on next page)

(continued from previous page)

Body part	Comfortable	Uncomfortable
Torso, chest, shoulders	▪ Leaning toward you ▪ Their torso is facing your torso	▪ Moving away from you ▪ Shielding their torso with object or hands ▪ Torso splaying (e.g., sprawling in a chair) is sign of disrespect ▪ Puffing up chest is sign of disrespect
Arms	▪ Unrestrained movement ▪ To relax someone, show inside of arms, palms up	▪ Arms across chest and/or coming down ▪ Arm freezing may indicate abuse
Touch	▪ Arms touching someone ▪ Brief touch on arm indicates ease	▪ Arms behind back
Hands and fingers	▪ Keeping hands in view ▪ Hand steepling	▪ Hiding hands ▪ Fingers pointing ▪ Shaking hands can indicate stress—depends on context ▪ Less movement when threatened ▪ Hand-wringing ▪ Thumbs in pockets, fingers out ▪ Interlacing of fingers ▪ Putting hands under the table
Face	▪ Loosening of forehead lines, lines around mouth relax, lips are fuller, eyes are wider	▪ Tense—tightening jaw, flared nostrils, quivering mouth, tight lips
Eyes	▪ Something we like—pupils dilate ▪ Eye flashes—a pleasant surprise	▪ Something we don't like—eyes constrict ▪ Eyes down—emotional processing ▪ Eye blocking ▪ Roving eyes leave a bad impression

Your autonomic nervous system is connected to your brain stem, which is your "survival brain." It is at the base of your skull. Your brain stem controls your motivation systems (food, sleep, sex, etc.) and your involuntary systems (eye blinking, saliva, heartbeat, etc.), and it is where you take your emotional hits (anything that jeopardizes safety or belonging). When you take an emotional hit, it goes down your spine, and your first reaction is to freeze, run, or fight.

When you believe your safety or belonging is jeopardized, your SNS is triggered. The fire alarm blares. Your heart rate goes up, your blood sugar goes up, and your muscles react. Your feet start moving, then your legs. The blood goes toward your torso and away from your hands, which get cold. Digestion stops, the immune system stops working—your whole body is on high alert.

When your whole body is on high alert, that impacts your thinking and responses.

Some basics about your brain

To understand the basic structure of the brain and the development of the emotional self, the "hand model" explained by Daniel Siegel is very helpful.[2]

Hand model of the brain

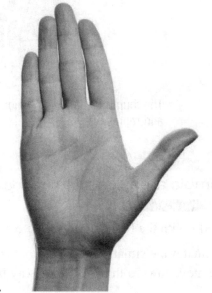

The palm is the brain stem, which controls the involuntary systems.

The wrist is the spinal cord.

The brain stem

- Controls our states of arousal—hungry, sexually aroused, awake, asleep
- Responsible for fight-or-flight response
- Identifies how we respond to threats; in survival mode, brain becomes reactive
- Fundamental to motivational systems that help

The limbic region

The thumb is the limbic region of the brain
and represents the amygdala

The limbic area (includes amygdala and hippocampus)

- Works with the brain stem to create our emotions
- Evaluates the situation—good (compassionate) or bad (uncompassionate)? We move toward the good and away from the bad

The limbic area (continued)

- Creates "e-motions"—the motion we choose (toward or away from) according to the meaning we assign to the situation

- Is crucial to how we form relationships and become emotionally attached to one another

- Regulates the hypothalamus—which is the endocrine control center; when we are stressed, we secrete a hormone that stimulates the adrenal glands to release cortisol, which mobilizes energy by putting our entire system on alert

- Is sensitized by trauma and then over-fires; "finding a way to soothe excessively reactive limbic firing is crucial to rebalancing emotions and diminishing the harmful effects of chronic stress"[3]

- Helps create memories—of facts, experiences, emotions

- Includes the amygdala, which is especially important in the fear response; "emotional responses can be created without consciousness and we may act on them without awareness"[4]

- Includes the hippocampus, which puts the puzzle pieces together; i.e., it is responsible for the integration of experiences—body sensations, emotions, thoughts, facts, recollections, etc.

The cortex

The back of the hand and the fingers over
the thumb represent the cortex of the brain.

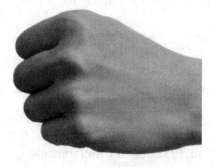 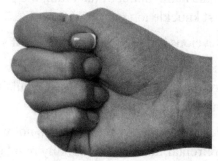

The cortex

- Is the outer layer of the brain
- The frontal cortex moves the brain beyond survival, bodily functions, and emotional reactions and into thoughts and ideas
- The frontal cortex creates its own representations—it allows us to think about thinking
- In the hand model of the brain, the frontal cortex extends from your fingertips to the second knuckle

The prefrontal cortex

The middle two fingers are the prefrontal cortex.

Adapted from D. J. Siegel, *Mindsight*

The prefrontal cortex

- In the hand model of the brain, the prefrontal cortex extends from your first knuckle to your fingertips
- Develops a sense of time, a sense of self, and moral judgments
- In the hand model of the brain, the two middle fingers are the middle prefrontal region—it controls impulsivity, has insight and empathy, and enacts moral judgments
- Because the prefrontal cortex is not well-developed in poverty,[5] "the nine prefrontal functions: (1) bodily regulation, (2) attuned communication, (3) emotional balance, (4) response flexibility, (5) fear modulation, (6) empathy, (7) insight, (8) moral awareness, and (9) intuition"[6] are also underdeveloped

Vertical integration

Put your thumb in the middle of your palm, and curl your fingers over the top. The back of the hand represents the back of your head. Your wrist is the spinal cord rising from your backbone, upon which your brain sits. The inner brain stem is your palm. Your thumb in your palm represents the limbic region of the brain. Your fingers curled over the top of your thumb represent your cortex.

The brain stem, the limbic area, and the cortex are what have been called "the triune brain." To integrate the brain means linking the activities of the brain stem, the limbic area, and the cortex. It means that these parts "talk" to each other.

This is called "vertical integration."

How your brain melts down:

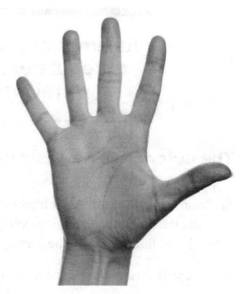

Using the hand model to illustrate, your thumb comes out and your fingers go up. Boom!

It is an in-your-face explosion!

The emotions are not regulated or integrated with the prefrontal cortex. The prefrontal cortex is the regulator. Your feelings are waving around out there unregulated. It is very easy for the fingers to fly up in the air and "explode."

Emotion is processed 200–5,000 times faster than thought.
–Steven Stosny, *The Powerful Self*[7]

Limbic lava: An emotional response just below the middle prefrontal area can explode into out-of-control activity. Hunger, fatigue, the meaning of an event—almost anything can trigger it. The middle prefrontal cortex is the part of the brain that "calms the reactive lower limbic and brain stem layers—[when it] stops being able to regulate all the energy being stirred up and the coordination and balance of the brain is disrupted…we flip our lids."[8]

It is the prefrontal cortex that keeps the amygdala "contained within the hand." When the brain is regulated and integrated in this way, the regulation and integration stop emotional meltdowns from occurring.

An emotional meltdown is an unregulated, unintegrated brain response.

The autonomic nervous system and the brain

When there is an emotional meltdown, the blood leaves the cortex and goes to the brain stem. The amygdala hijacks the cortex, and the person reacts. This activates the sympathetic nervous system. On average, it takes 25–30 minutes before blood flow returns to the cortex.

It is essential to calm the other person or yourself before having a conversation.

What are calming techniques?

a. **Water**—Give the person a bottle of water. Water helps the body metabolize cortisol, which is produced when someone gets physically upset. When the shoulders relax, the water has been effective in metabolizing the cortisol.

b. **Tapping and touch**—Tapping is based upon the energy system of the body. Western medicine has focused on the chemical part of the body (pharmaceuticals and surgery). Traditional Eastern medicine focuses on the energy system of the body (meridians and chakras). If you have had acupuncture, you have used the energy system. For more information about this, read the book *Tapping the Healer Within* by Richard Trubo and Roger Callahan, or watch videos on emotional freedom techniques. Adults use tapping to lose weight, stop smoking, go to sleep, calm themselves down, etc.

c. **Look up**—Simply making the eyes go upward by looking at the ceiling can help calm people who are having an emotional meltdown—especially if they are crying. When eyes are up across the top of the head, the brain is processing visual information. When eyes are moving between the ears, the brain is processing auditory information. When eyes are down, the brain tends to be processing emotional or kinesthetic information. The anecdotal evidence is that looking up makes it more difficult (or even impossible) to access emotion.

A little more about how you got your amygdala and hippocampus

Your emotional self (amygdala) is highly developed by the time you are three years old, and it is developed basically before you have language. So, you act on information you don't know you have. If you have ever done something and then said to yourself, "That is just like my mother (or father)," you are using information you got very young.

At birth, you have trillions of pieces of data coming at you all at once, and so you have to sort. You are sorting on the basis of these questions: Is it safe? Do I belong? Do I like it or not? Emotions are fairly simple. They are made of energy and motion, and to remember this you can think of them as "e-motions." You are either moving toward something or moving away from it. You smell milk, you like it, you like the person who holds you, you move toward them. You don't like something, you don't like someone, you move away from them. And that is how a person begins to structure what has meaning for them, which relationships are important to them.

The amygdala holds the emotional self and dictates which "e-motions" you'll make. Part of the way it does this is by releasing the hormone cortisol. Cortisol creates anxiety.

At the time of the September 11 terror attacks in 2001, there were 1,700 pregnant women directly affected by the collapse of the World Trade Center. Some of these women and their babies were included in a research study that found one indicator of PTSD was passed from the mothers to the children. Children of mothers who developed PTSD, especially the ones whose mothers were in the third trimester of their pregnancies at the time of attack, had cortisol levels that correlate with PTSD.[9] This means they may suffer from increased anxiety all their lives. This is the study of epigenetics—how the environment can change the way your genes are expressed. Epigenetic changes do not alter your DNA sequence, but they do change the way your body "reads" DNA. Epigenetic changes are heritable and can be present for generations. Luckily, epigenetic changes are reversible via healthy diet, lifestyle choices, and other interventions.

Your hippocampus is where you keep the story of who you are. McLean's research found that if you cannot keep a coherent story across time (past, present, future) and across contexts (work, school, home), then you may suffer from depression, PTSD, etc.[10]

Back to safety and belonging at work

If your workplace is a place where you do not feel safety or belonging, find another job. It is possible to have a job or career where danger is present (law enforcement, for example) yet feel safety and belonging with colleagues. Bonding occurs with colleagues because of the need to function together to stay safe. However, if there is no safety and no belonging, then the workplace hypersensitizes the SNS. It is as if the SNS is permanently in the "on" position. When that happens, then the body is not able to keep physically healthy because the PNS (which regulates rest and digestion) is not functioning.

Differences among colleagues

What makes you feel unsafe may not be the same as what makes your colleagues or boss feel unsafe. Individual differences occur along the way, and this will be discussed in the next chapter.

A story from Ruby

I had a director's position in a school district that had a superintendent who was charismatic, charming, intelligent, and unethical. He would tell you something, and then five minutes later, in a meeting, he would say just the opposite.

One day he called me and asked me to do something illegal with the funds for which I was responsible—a violation of federal law. I knew that if I did it, I could go to jail for it, and so did he. I also knew that if I told him no, he would write me up for insubordination.

So, I said to him, "I would be glad to do that if you will give me the directive in writing and sign your name to it." He never did that.

Being in that workplace made me uneasy, but I had safety and belonging with my colleagues. They had my back. I was part of a team that was ethical and fabulous to work with, so I had safety and belonging at that level.

How to apply this information in your workplace

What are the things that make you uneasy at work?

1.

2.

3.

Where or with whom do you have safety and belonging in the workplace?

1.

2.

3.

Do you have safety and belonging outside of work? With whom? Your family? Your siblings? Your spouse or significant other? Your children?

1.

2.

3.

Conclusion

Safety and belonging are critical to your emotional well-being. They keep your SNS and PNS in balance, which keeps you physically healthier also.

Journaling questions and prompts

- In what situation in your life do you feel the safest?

- Write about a time in your past when you felt like you didn't belong.

- The initial response to feeling unsafe or like you don't belong comes from the nonconscious part of your mind. It spreads from your brain throughout your body and causes you to take some kind of action (fight, flight, or freeze).

  - Where does tension about safety and belonging show up in your body?

  - Do you tend more toward fight, flight, or freeze? When you think about your instinctive reactions, what emotions do you experience?

- By the time your brain has gone through the initial reaction to a potentially unsafe situation, your thinking brain (prefrontal cortex) is playing catch-up. Our brains want to keep us safe—physically at first, and then by explaining the world in a way that makes sense and makes life predictable. What are the go-to stories you tell yourself about situations in which you have reacted to feeling unsafe or like you do not belong? Do you tend toward blaming others? ("What is wrong with that guy?") Do you often internalize responsibility? ("What did I do wrong this time?")

- Make two columns on a piece of paper. In the first column, write messages that the voice of shame speaks to you. In the second column, write true responses to counter the voice of shame. For example:

Shame's message	Truth
You don't belong here, and you will never be able to connect with these people.	Working relationships are challenging, and there will be conflict. But everyone here is in the same boat as me, and we are all doing our best. We can figure it out.

Discussion questions for staff

- Our brains are constantly scanning the environment at a nonconscious level for cues about safety and belonging. This is one of the reasons your first impression is so important in working with people, especially people who are in need. People's nonconscious brains read nonverbal cues in a new setting before any conversation has started. What is the first meeting like for the people we serve? What about these other kinds of contact they have with us?

  - Phone: Text or voice? Is the automated system easy to use? What is the tone of voice of those who answer the phones?

  - In-person reception: What are the nonverbals of staff members like? Are they dressed in accordance with company guidelines? Is there a clear process for customers? Is the signage direct and easy to follow?

  - Second-level interactions: What happens on the way from reception to the customer's destination?

  - Home visits: Do you visit customers at home?

- ◆ Regardless of the outcome of any given interaction, is a visit with us viewed as "good news"? Are the people we serve glad we are part of their lives?

- Staff conversations that happen in the presence of the people being served are strong indicators of the level of safety that exists in an organization. Schools are especially notorious for adult-to-adult conversations the adults think students are not hearing, seeing, or being impacted by. How are we doing with staff-to-staff conversations that happen near our customers? How do we talk about staff who are not present?

- How can we practice assuming positive intent on the part of others? When we assume people's intentions are positive, how does that affect the way we deal with each other and with clients/customers? Conflict starts with initial reactions to behaviors we don't understand. What can we do to mediate those first reactions and create a stronger sense of safety and belonging?

Activities to explore

Body scan

This activity is a way to become more familiar and more comfortable with the way your body communicates stress.

Sit in a comfortable position. Close your eyes and take a few slow breaths. Starting at your feet, focus on each part of your body and notice any physical discomfort. The purpose of this activity is to notice, not to fix or change anything. As you become more familiar with the way your brain sends a message through your body, you can recognize possible stress before it hijacks your thinking and actions. Do this brief activity every day for 4–6 weeks. You will be training your brain to better interpret your reactions.

Scan the following:

- Feet to knees

- Knees to hips

- Lower torso

- Upper torso

- Shoulders and neck

- Head

Grounding in the present: Sensory scan

When our brain stem and limbic system are reacting, our brain collapses the time between the present event and the events that first caused us to react in that way. Implicit memory can affect our thoughts and behaviors unconsciously, without us recalling any particular event from the past. In other words, our implicit memories can bring emotions from the past into the present even though the current situation has nothing to do with the situation in the past. People who have undergone significant trauma sometimes experience flashbacks, or explicit memories, in which the trauma seems to be occurring in the present moment. If significant trauma is part of your background, please seek professional support if you haven't done so already, as activities like the sensory scan and others found here are not designed to replace therapeutic work with qualified professionals.

Shame may tell you that trauma is best left in the past, or perhaps that it's a secret no one can know. Shame is lying to you. Sharing your secrets, while very frightening, brings relief. Secrets keep showing up, particularly in the form of implicit memories. Sharing secrets with a trusted friend or counselor helps you to recognize implicit memories before they have a chance to hijack your current reactions and thinking.

This activity can be done sitting or standing. It is a way to bring yourself back into the present moment while also acknowledging the reality of the emotions you are experiencing. After taking a couple deep breaths, notice things in your environment that you can see, hear, taste, touch, and smell. Note that each of these things are in the "here and now."

- I can smell the coffee in the coffee pot.

- I can hear the sound of people having conversations.

- I see the desk in my office.

- I can touch this book that is in front me.

- I can taste this apple on my desk.

As you do this sensory scan, you are using parts of your brain that require thinking and language. This assists you in integrating your brain. The point is not to eliminate the emotion or the stress—at least not at first. The point is to bring your experience into the present moment.

Practice breathing

Slow, deep breathing is a useful tool for bringing the sympathetic and parasympathetic nervous systems into balance. Learning to control your breathing during stressful situations can help keep you in control of your reactions. You don't have to do this for 20 minutes; just a few slow, deep breaths will train your body and become a habit you can use.

One thing you can do is to recognize the balance of the SNS and PNS in your pulse while you are breathing. As you inhale, your heart rate will increase (SNS). As you exhale, your heart rate will decrease. A strategy for deep breathing is to breathe out slowly for a longer period than you breathed in. This assists your body in going to the PNS and managing the fire alarm of the SNS.

Chapter Two

Developing Relationships in the Workplace

Who are your favorite people at work? With whom do you have the best relationships?

1.

2.

3.

What is attachment theory?

Before you were one year old, you had already developed your style of bonding and attachment. There are four styles of bonding and attachment. People can also have bonding and attachment disorders, but here we'll discuss only the different styles of bonding and attachment. These styles follow you into your working relationships, romantic relationships, and friendships.

John Bowlby is the originator of attachment theory. He says the following:

> When a baby is born, he cannot tell one person from another...yet by his first birthday, he...[can] distinguish familiars from strangers...and chooses one or more favorites...Their loss causes anxiety and distress; their recovery, relief and a sense of security. On this foundation, it seems, the rest of his emotional life is built—without this foundation there is risk for his future happiness and health.[11]

If you would like to identify your own bonding and attachment style, there are many quizzes available online.

Bonding and attachment is the process by which the brain becomes integrated and regulated. It is also the process by which inner strengths and weaknesses are initially developed.

Bowlby's work was concerned with attachment to the caregiver, and he focused on the effects of separation and loss across the life span.[12]

Mary Ainsworth, a developmental psychologist who worked with Bowlby, came up with the most widely accepted method for measuring attachment in infants—the Strange Situation, sometimes called the Infant Strange Situation.[13]

Ainsworth theorized that a way to know that a child had a secure sense of self was to see whether the child would feel comfortable exploring without losing the sense of safety and belonging. To research this, the researchers filled a room with toys. They would watch the child explore the space while the caregiver was nearby. Then they would have a stranger walk into the room. They watched the child's response. Then the caregiver would leave the room, and the child was alone with the stranger. Then the infants were watched for their reactions to separation and reunion with their caregiver.

The research of Bowlby, Ainsworth, and others eventually identified four styles of bonding and attachment. Before we get into the styles, please note that some disorders may impact the bonding and attachment style. Autism spectrum disorder and other conditions, especially when untreated, can make the bonding and attachment style seem disorganized when it's actually secure and attached.

The four styles of bonding and attachment

Secure and attached	Insecure and anxious-ambivalent
Insecure and anxious-avoidant	Disorganized (safe and dangerous)

Attachment theory asks: "Are you bonded to a caregiver? Is that bond secure or insecure? And what kind of a self did you develop?" Secure means that you believe you are safe. Attached means that you believe you belong. Note again that there are bonding and attachment disorders. This information is only about bonding and attachment styles.

In the Strange Situation experiment, when the child had secure attachment, the child often cried when the mother left, actively greeted her when she returned (often showing some physical response), and then returned to play and exploration. The caregiver was attuned to the child's needs, and *the child's sense of self was secure and integrated.*

Children who had anxious-avoidant attachment focused on toys or exploring the room and showed no signs of distress when the caregiver left or returned. The caregiver did not respond to the child's signals in a reliable or sensitive manner. In return, the child minimized activation of the attachment circuitry in the brain. *The child's sense of self was disconnected.*

When the caregiver was inconsistent, the child experienced anxious-ambivalent attachment. The child seemed distressed before the separation and looked for the caregiver upon return, but the child was not readily soothed and may have continued to cry. The caregiver did not give the child a sense of relief. The attachment circuitry was overactivated. *The child's sense of self was confused.*

Disorganized—safe and dangerous—attachment occurs when caregivers are unattuned to the needs of the child, are frightening to the child, and are often frightened themselves. The child cannot find any effective means to cope and develops no attachment strategy. *The child's sense of self is fragmented, unregulated, and unintegrated.*

According to Stosny, disorganized attachment occurs in about 10% of the general population but in up to 80% of high-risk groups such as the children of drug-addicted parents. It is quite upsetting to watch the child when the parent returns. The infant may look terrified, approach and then withdraw, freeze or fall to the floor, cling or cry while pulling away. The parent is unpredictable—sometimes safe and sometimes dangerous.

People whose bonding and attachment style is disorganized are often very dismissive of people. Their attachments are variable: sometimes safe, sometimes dangerous. For example, when they were growing up, if they never knew whether they were going to be slapped or kissed, they couldn't put anything together about themselves, and they couldn't put stock in attachments to others.

The following stories show how a child's bonding and attachment to a caregiver can be disorganized and disoriented because the adult is sometimes safe and sometimes dangerous. The effect of this is that the child may learn to be safe and dangerous too.

A story: Bad news—Dave

Dave had a father who was a self-made multimillionaire. Until Dave was 10 years old, Dave and his father were the best of buddies. When Dave went to middle school, because Dave's grades were not as good as the father wanted them to be, he started a file on Dave. The title of the file was "Bad News—Dave." The father left it on his desk where his son could see it and added to the list each time Dave did something the father did not like. Dave stated that he was so confused at that age because he could not figure out why all of a sudden he was "bad news."

The criticism and shame continued throughout adolescence. Dave was expected to stay at home and babysit younger siblings while his parents partied on the weekends. As an adult, Dave struggled with relationships; in particular, he chose romantic relationships where the partner reinforced the idea that he was "bad news." His father was physically safe but psychologically dangerous.

Bonding and attachment occurs intensely twice during childhood: in infancy (birth to three) and then again in adolescence, when the brain is making significant changes (both pruning and developing parts of the brain). The bonding and attachment of the child to an adult impacts the child's emotional well-being for the rest of the child's life.

A parent can be safe and dangerous in any of these ways: sexually, physically, emotionally, verbally, psychologically, etc. A parent can be very safe for the first bonding of the infant but be both safe and dangerous when the child is an adolescent and can think independently.

What does having a safe and dangerous parent do to the child?

As an infant, the child's sense of self is fragmented. Who they are as a self is not developed, and the child becomes both safe and dangerous—out of control—in total reaction to those nearby.

Four bonding and attachment styles in detail

Secure and attached

*Person's sense of self
is integrated and secure*

- Are not easily influenced by peers
- Tend to do better academically
- Form healthy relationships
- Brain tends to be integrated and regulated

*"I'm lovable, and you will find
my love worth having."*[14]

Insecure, anxious-ambivalent

*Person's sense of
self is confused*

- Very anxious in the workplace
- Often easily bullied
- Difficulty with boundaries in relationships
- Do not always do the work because it might not be right
- Need repeated assurances
- Self is to blame if there is a relationship problem

*"I'm not lovable, but you are so
loving that I will do anything to
get you to stay/like me."*[15]

Insecure, anxious-avoidant

*Person's sense of self
is disconnected*

- Tend to be loners
- Difficulty with forming relationships
- Are restricted emotionally
- Avoid situations that require an emotional response
- Peers often do not like them

*"I am unlovable and you'll reject
me anyway, so why bother."*[16]

Disorganized
(safe and dangerous)

*Person's sense of self is
fragmented, unregulated,
and unintegrated*

- Operate out of fear and anger
- Cannot name their emotions
- Have parents who are often safe and dangerous and tend to rage when angry
- Few boundaries, little attachment
- Have no compassion for others

*"I'm lovable, but you're either too
insensitive to see it or you're just
not worthy of my love."*[17]

Stosny, a researcher and clinician, works with men who batter women. He indicates that the disorganized (safe and dangerous) style of attachment is "disproportionally represented." He goes on to say that "the most violent people in intimate relationships will be young children and young men."[18]

Will the parents' own bonding and attachment experience impact their children?

Yes and no. If the adults cannot form a coherent life narrative from the experiences they have had, the answer is that their bonding and attachment experience tends to be repeated.

"The best predictor of a child's security of attachment is not what happened to his parents as children, but rather *how his parents made sense of those childhood experiences.*"[19]

The key to making sense is a life narrative. For example, adults whose children develop secure bonding and attachment tend to see both the positive and negative aspects of their development and how that contributed to who they are. They are able to see the adults in their childhoods through the eyes of an adult and not those of a child.

"The best predictor of a child's security of attachment is not what happened to his parents as children, but rather how his parents made sense of those childhood experiences."

How does feeling "less than" and "separate from" create anger, anxiety, avoidance, resentment, shame, guilt, humiliation, violence, and revenge?

When bonding and attachment is not secure and the inner self is weak, then the brain is not integrated and regulated. The result may be anger, anxiety, rage, revenge, and violence.

There is a process that is repeated over and over again in life. It is a process of bonding, then separation, then individuation, and then new bonding. The infant bonds to the caregiver, then the child turns two years old and the answer to everything is suddenly "no" (this is separation). Then the child learns to be an individual person in relationship to another person—develops a sense of self (this is individuation). Then the child moves on to new friends. This process repeats in adolescence, in early adulthood, and all through life.

The repeat process of life: Bonding, separation, individuation

Wherever there is a white line around the circle, this indicates there is emotional work to do. If the separations come too fast or are initiated by someone else, then the necessary grieving and mourning do not happen. Instead, it becomes compound grief.

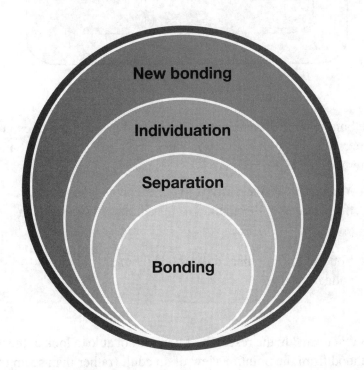

When the grief work does not happen, over time one becomes "boxed in."

"Boxed in" is where anger, resentment, violence, revenge, addiction, and anxiety begin to play key roles in the person's everyday life.

If you do not like your own style of bonding and attachment, what can you do?

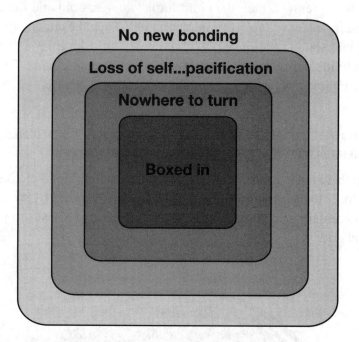

The bonding and attachment style you had growing up does not matter. The research is that you can change the impact of it and patterns you use if:

1. You can make a narrative of your life that clearly identifies the positives and negatives of the adults and situations in your life.

2. You can find another adult who will bond with you and validate you.

What does that mean? In the research, if you are not able to look at the adults in your childhood from the point of view of an adult (rather than seeing them as you did when you were the child in the parent–child relationship)—identifying both their assets and liabilities—and identify the core hurts and core values you received from them, then it is not possible for you to leave emotional poverty because you will be blindsided by the core hurts. It is analogous to having a festering sore that never heals, and if it gets bumped, it bleeds all over again.

The anxiety-ridden individual has lots of blame for the adults. There is a cartoon in which a woman is forcing her husband and children to help roll a huge ball of manure up a steep hill. It keeps rolling back to the bottom of the hill. Her husband says to her, "Can't we just leave it here at the bottom of the hill?"

His wife says, "No. My mother gave it to me, and I can't leave it alone."

Avoidant individuals are very dismissive of the experiences of others. They may say:

- "If I made it through, so can you."

- "We got beaten nearly every day by my mother, but it was good for us."

- "Yeah, my old man beat up on me, but I am okay."

If you don't want to react without knowing why, then here is a challenge:

1. On this timeline, identify five key memories/events/happenings in your life. For example: a death, marriage, birth of a child, college, groom did not show to my wedding, major car accident, Ms. Benton my fourth-grade teacher, homecoming queen, etc. Put an X on the timeline for each one. Label it if you wish. (Research indicates that individual personality is fairly shaped by 29 years of age.)

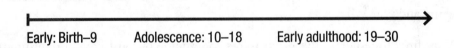

Early: Birth–9   Adolescence: 10–18   Early adulthood: 19–30

2. On this timeline, identify the five key people in your life who shaped your core self. Use initials to identify them.

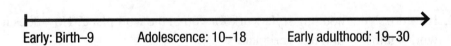

Early: Birth–9   Adolescence: 10–18   Early adulthood: 19–30

3. For each X in Question 1, identify the core inner hurts and core inner values you got from each X.

4. For each set of initials in Question 2, identify the core inner hurts and core inner values you received from each person.

Inner hurts	Inner values
• Less than	• Importance
• Separate from	• Value
• Disregarded	• Worthiness
• Unlovable	• Equality
• Accused	• Flexibility
• Rejected	• Resilience
• Powerless	• Ability to recognize core values in others
• Inadequate	
• Unimportant	

What triggers a reaction in us is a core hurt we did not know we had.

Identifying these hurts helps avoid a reaction we do not want to have.

The same inner hurts tend to show up repeatedly. Those are your triggers. When you are faced with anything that makes the amygdala think that your current experience is similar to a past experience, those same inner hurts will surface again, and you will react.

What fires together in the brain wires together. You will have an automatic response because that neural pathway is already established.

How to apply this information in your workplace

1. Who do you bond with at work the most?

2. How does your bonding style work for you in the workplace? How does it work against you in the workplace?

Journaling questions and prompts

• While most of us want to be secure in our attachment and bonding, even if we are, we tend toward one or the other of the insecure styles. Take some time to reflect on your own attachment style in terms of insecurities. Do you tend to be more ambivalent, seeking attention and affirmation? Or do you tend to be more avoidant, pulling away from others or even isolating?

- Write about the people at work who are easy for you to connect with and those who are more difficult to connect with. What specific characteristics of each relationship stand out for you? How do these relationships with coworkers remind you of family relationships or friendships from your past?

- In our work serving others, we would like to believe we are there for the clients/customers, not the other way around. But human interactions do not really work that way. They are a two-way street. Write about what you expect and need in your relationships with both coworkers and clients/customers.

Discussion questions for staff

- We all have three voices: adult, parent, and child. These three voices all have purpose and usefulness, but when we are building relationships with those we serve, the adult voice is essential, especially for those with an insecure bonding and attachment style. However, the tendency in service organizations and managerial situations is to default to the parent voice because it's the voice that tells people what they need to do. The problem is that the parent voice can be uncomfortable for those who did not have a consistently positive experience with adults in their family or at school. The parent voice becomes patronizing as well, because it speaks from a position of "I know and you don't." As a staff, do we stay in the adult voice when dealing with those we serve? How often do we default to the parent voice?

- Whole organizations can have a bonding and attachment tone. What bonding and attachment style is most reflected in the overall tone of our workplace?

- Consider your first interaction with clients/customers. A key sense of belonging comes from the experience of delight. We express delight with our eyes, face, voice, etc. when we are glad to see someone. It is automatic with people we love and care about. Do we delight in each other at work? Do those who access our services feel that we delight in them?

Activities to explore

- Go deeper with the timeline activity. Write down as many significant relational events as you can think of from your childhood and adolescence. What did each of these contribute to your bonding and attachment? This activity is best done with a trusted other, perhaps a friend who is interested in doing the same activity. Telling stories to a compassionate listener is powerful in addressing the negative stories from our past and the voice of shame that comes from those stories.

- Earned secure attachment is when a person with an insecure attachment style is involved in a relationship of mutual respect that essentially rewires the brain to believe that secure attachment is possible. This can happen in childhood or with adult relationships. Earned secure attachment is the result of the relationship, not the relationship itself. Consider the relationships in your life that have reinforced a secure attachment style. Secure attachment is formed when there is a rupture in the relationship followed by a repair. For example, a parent might frustrate their children by limiting their behavior (by saying no), but then the parent assists them in moving through the frustration. The relationship is bigger than the incident, and each incident ends well. We can replicate this process of rupture and repair in adult relationships and help ourselves and others experience more secure attachment—a deeper sense of safety and belonging.

- Our brains are amazing in their ability to develop new neurological pathways even in the area of bonding and attachment. Three things that have been shown to improve neuroplasticity are aerobic exercise, new learning, and focused attention activities such as puzzles, word games, etc. Develop a plan to increase these things in your life.

Chapter Three

What Motivates Behavior? Strong and Weak Inner Selves, Emotional Assets, and Liabilities at Work

The motivation for desirable behavior is a strong inner self.

The amygdala is that part of the brain that is so critical in emotional strength and emotional meltdowns—but how does it develop? How do we construct a self? How does an inner self get formed?

Birth to age three

The first steps in self-construction occur from birth to age three. A second burst of self-construction comes during adolescence, when the brain prunes, reorganizes, and establishes new neural pathways. From birth to age three, almost all of the neural pathways are new.

What is self-construction?

Core self-evaluations are important in self-construction. They are a characteristic of a stable personality that includes a person's subconscious and their essential assessment of themselves and their abilities. People with high core self-evaluations think positively of themselves and are confident in their abilities. People with low core self-evaluations view themselves negatively and are insecure.[20]

> The term "self-construction" is a rubric for a set of beliefs, feelings, and behaviors about the self that form the perspective from which individuals construct meaning. *Self-constructions make up the unique*

lens through which each individual sees the world. In fact, the brain processes information about the world—gives it meaning—according to how it constructs the self.[21]

Self-construction builds the inner self. What the inner self does is sort through billions of stimuli to construct a world that is in agreement with the self-construction. "Although the brain is always changing, the limbic system [which includes the amygdala] is pretty much fully developed on a structural level by age three. Hence, it is called the *Toddler brain.*"[22]

When you are an infant, the caregivers and key adults around you point out stimuli to which you should pay attention. As an infant, you do not know what is dangerous, how to feed yourself, or how to take care of yourself. The actions and admonitions of the adults around you are factored into the development of the inner self.

Developmental psychologist and psychoanalyst Erik Erikson developed the most widely accepted theory of human psychological development. Erikson outlines the stages of development and how the inner self gets developed—both in healthy ways and in less-than-healthy ways. Erikson says psychosocial strength, what we're calling inner strength, "depends on a total process which regulates individual life cycles, the sequence of generations, and the structure of society simultaneously, for all three have evolved together."[23]

Erikson's stages of development and the associated ages are not prescriptive but rather descriptive and approximate. Depending upon the individual, some developmental stages may occur earlier or later. Erikson outlines the kind of development that needs to occur for a strong inner self.

Each stage has a range of development that can be expressed as a continuum. For example, trust and distrust: It is possible to develop trust or distrust at this stage, depending upon the nature of the relationship and the child's external environment. People can also fall anywhere along the continuum; some people are more trusting than others, and some people are more distrustful than others.

Erikson's stages of psychosocial development

Age	Range of development	Tasks and relationships in that development
First six months	Continuum: Trust ←--→ distrust Trust of others and self	• Mother or caregiver • "Basic trust [is] the cornerstone of a vital personality"[24] • Trust gives a sense of being okay—that one can trust oneself—that always remains subliminally all of one's life
Second six months	Continuum: Trust ←--→ distrust Trust of others and self	• Focus on sensory information, the self as an individual, and the dependence on the environment—particularly the mother, who periodically attends to other issues besides the child • If the child interprets the mother's absence as withdrawal instead of trust, the infant develops distrust • This trust is built not upon the quantity of time with the mother but the quality
Years 2 and 3	Continuum: Autonomy ←--→ shame Shame includes self-doubt	• Child can either hang on or let go • "For the child, controlling the bowel movement is a significant step towards autonomy"[25] • Child uses *I, you, my* • Obedient or rebellious • Shame and doubt come if the child is made fun of, cannot reach goals, and/or if parents prove to be unpredictable • Child needs to be protected from too many failures • Shame is "rage turned against the self," and "doubt is the brother of shame"[26] • If the child is not allowed to develop autonomy, then the child can develop self-doubt and compulsive behavior • Autonomy/shame shows up in the individual's relationship to law and order

(continued on next page)

Erikson's stages of psychosocial development (continued)

Age	Range of development	Tasks and relationships in that development
Years 4 and 5	Continuum: Initiative ←–→ guilt	• Shifts focus from self to the environment • Notices similarities and differences • Develops curiosity and motivation to do something • Language and locomotion permit exploration and imagination[27] • Compares self to adults • Intrusive—into new space, into adult minds and conversations, into the unknown • Develops a conscience—beginning development of morality • Develops a fear of losing, loss • If this stage is not fully developed, it will hamper and restrict initiative later in life; source of apathy if child learns it's not safe to try things • Contributes to identity development later in life by freeing the initiative to do adult tasks and develop one's own abilities
Year 6 to puberty	Continuum: Industry ←–→ inferiority	• "Growing need to be productive, to learn something new, to contribute to the world of adults and to be recognized by it"[28] • "Growing abilities to watch, to join, to observe, and to participate"[29] • Play becomes very important—"allows the child a new level of coping with reality"[30] • Adults see play as a means to escape reality; for children, it is a means to cope with reality[31] • Can get appreciation from others by doing or learning things independently • If trying again is not encouraged by a role model, the child may develop a deep sense of being a failure • Continuous failure, fear-based teaching methods, and solely performance-based acceptance may lead to feelings of inferiority

(continued on next page)

Erikson's stages of psychosocial development (continued)

Age	Range of development	Tasks and relationships in that development
Puberty to Year 18	Continuum: Identity ← - → role confusion	• Pathway between childhood and adulthood • Rapid body growth and genital maturity • Key question is: "How am I seen by others?" • The adolescent goes through a phase of upheaval similar to the one in infancy; in addition, there is the need for recognition from the outside, though for now recognition by peers is of prime importance • Here the goal is to find own identity through the negation of generally accepted values and norms • When there is no sense of identity, then there is role confusion; role confusion is a conflict within one's own personality • Defined identity is a precondition for intimacy
Year 19 to early adulthood	Continuum: Intimacy ← - → self-centeredness	• Building sustainable relationships and friendships; capacity for intimacy • Personality formation is mostly complete • Development of an ethical sense • Individual can regulate intimate connections while also regulating work, procreation, and recreation • If intimacy is avoided, "may settle for highly stereotyped interpersonal relations and come to retain a deep sense of isolation"[32] • If intimacy has not been developed sufficiently, the consequence is often isolation, leading to psychic disorders, depressive self-absorption, or vulnerable characteristics

What does this mean in the workplace?

Stages	Stronger self-construction	Less developed self-construction
First year of life Trust ← – → distrust	• Individuals tend to trust leadership and see authority as a way to keep safe • Tend to do what the leader asks • Tend to follow organizational guidelines	• Individuals are distrusting of authority
Ages 2 and 3 Autonomy ← – → shame	• I can do the tasks • I can take care of and be responsible for me • I can ask for help	• May be unwilling to try for fear of failure • May develop compulsive behavior to avoid the self-doubt • May see themselves as victims • Very sensitive to criticism or failure
Ages 4 and 5 Initiative ← – → guilt	• Are motivated to try and learn new things • Curious about many things	• May be apathetic if it's not safe to try things • May develop a fear of losing, so will not try
Ages 6 to puberty Industry ← – → inferiority	• Are willing to put effort into the task • Like getting appreciation from others • Like to do things by themselves	• If no positive role model present to encourage, will often quit • Fear-based mandates increase feelings of inferiority • Will quit if they believe they are failures
Puberty to 18 Identity ← – → role confusion	• Have the recognition of peers • Have a sense of who they are • Have a sense of a future story	• Role confusion; not sure who they are • Often bullied • Hard to have a future story when you are not sure about yourself
18 to 29 (adult personality is formed by then) Intimacy ← – → self-centeredness	• Have sustainable relationships with adults and peers • Respond to an ethical sense	• Relationships are more temporary and changeable • May develop a deep sense of isolation • May be depressed or vulnerable

All of these stages are instrumental in developing the inner self. It is difficult to get to self-identity if earlier stages are not developed.

Weak and strong inner self

If one develops more on the stronger side—trust, autonomy, initiative, industry, identity, and intimacy—then the inner self engages in the behavior that evidences that. If one develops more on the weaker side—distrust, shame, guilt, inferiority, role confusion, and social isolation—then the inner self engages in the behavior that evidences that. This then becomes the motivation for the behavior.

Inner hurts	Inner strengths
• Less than	• Importance
• Separate from	• Value
• Disregarded	• Worthiness
• Unlovable	• Equality
• Accused	• Flexibility
• Rejected	• Resilience
• Powerless	• Compassion
• Inadequate	
• Unimportant	

Emotional age versus chronological age

Every person has an emotional age and a chronological age. If you have ever made the comment, "He is 40 but he acts like he is 18," you have made a distinction between emotional age and chronological age. Psychologists indicate that at whatever age the abuse or trauma occurred or the addiction began, that is where the emotional development stops until they either get therapy or a nurturing, caring adult.

Emotional assets and liabilities

Emotional assets are often referred to as emotional intelligence or "soft skills." There is a saying in the human resources business: "Hire on skills, fire on behavior." The "fire on behavior" part of the saying refers to what can happen when emotional liabilities show up. Emotional liabilities tend to be based on inner hurts and the need to address those.

For example, if you developed more distrust than trust, you will find it difficult to trust authority and will tend not to do what your leadership asks. You do not believe that leadership is to be trusted. Failure to follow requests from leadership often is seen as a liability, an undesirable behavior by management.

Genetic basis of personality

Does personality have a genetic basis? Yes, it does. Both autism and anxiety have a genetic basis. Also, psychologists have identified the "big five" personality traits that have a genetic basis and seem to be fairly universal.

Big five personality traits

1. Agreeableness (compassion and politeness)
2. Conscientiousness (industriousness and orderliness)
3. Extraversion (enthusiasm and assertiveness)
4. Neuroticism (withdrawal and volatility)
5. Openness to experience (openness and intellect)

There are many self-assessments online that can show you how strongly you exhibit each of these personality traits.[33]

Develop more desirable behavior using the process of validation

Validation is the process by which you move an individual from a weak inner self to a strong inner self.

It is very difficult to change a behavior. To change a behavior, change the motivation for the behavior.

Here is what happens in the motivation of good behavior: When people experience something that taps an inner hurt, they are able to realize that this behavior or comment reflects more on the other person than on themselves. The brain is regulated and integrated, and a strong inner self is tapped.

People in this position either do not respond, or they respond calmly and without anger. This allows them to see the situation with compassion and to use validation if possible. In future interactions with the individual who triggered the inner hurt, they are able to identify appropriate boundaries, consequences, or support.

What is the protocol for validation?

Validation

- Calm the individual.

- Help identify the deep hurt.

- Help identify the ways in which the deep hurt is not true.

- Visit the thinking of the other person involved.

- Identify the deep value/strengths the individual has.

- Identify the consequences for the behavior.

- Examine other choices for the future.

A story from Ruby

When I was a beginning consultant, I was the youngest consultant in the organization. My boss, Gerald, gave me a project to lead the first week I was on the job. Two of the senior consultants came to me and told me that I did not have the expertise or experience to lead the project. Not wanting to create animosity and wanting to be a team player, I suggested we work together on the project.

The senior consultants took the leadership away from me and excluded me. Within a couple of days, I realized what had happened but did not know what to do about it.

About five days after Gerald gave me the job, he called me in and asked what had happened. I explained and apologized.

Here is how he validated me and the situation: First, he asked me what happened. Then he helped me identify the deep hurt. I explained that I did not want to create adversarial relationships.

Then he helped identify the ways in which the deep hurt was not true, and he let me in on his own thinking. He said to me, "I am an old basketball coach. I am the coach. I gave you the ball to play. You do not listen to the taunts from the other team or from players on your own team. I am the coach. It is your job to play the ball. I gave you the ball to play."

He then identified my deep strengths. "I gave you the ball to play because you have abilities I needed to put into the game. You have the ability to 'smell' what we are going to need before we need it."

Then he went to the consequence. "The next time I give you the ball to play, I want you to play it. Let me worry about the other players. You play the ball."

He could have written me up for the mistake. He could have reprimanded me. Instead, he validated me with a consequence. I have never forgotten his example.

When the behavior must be managed because it cannot be changed

There are also situations where the behavior cannot be changed but must instead be managed.

In situations where the behavior must be managed, it is important to note that a process must be in place for constant monitoring of that individual and adaptation of the interventions.

Keep consequences in place; change the approach.

How to apply this information in your workplace

1. Using this chart, identify where you fall on the inner self continuum. It often depends on the situation.

Situation	Inner hurt that shows up	Inner strength that shows up

For example, I, Ruby, grew up in a closed, religious environment that did not allow girls or women to participate in sports. So, when that stage of industry versus performance—when I would have been learning athletic skills—is tapped, I can only evidence inferiority. When someone says to me as an adult, "Let's play volleyball," I turn into a six-year-old and make up a reason I cannot be there.

2. What emotional assets and liabilities do you bring to the workplace? What situations do you avoid? What irritates you? What do you do well? What situations do you not handle well?

Journaling questions and prompts

- Make a list of the words you use to describe yourself when you are upset, angry, frustrated, sad, etc. Often those words reflect inner hurts. They also often are the voice of shame. For each of the words, write a better response, one that you would be comfortable giving to another person or a child dealing with the same negative thoughts.

- Compassion for others starts with self-compassion. Develop a self-talk script for when you are stressed.

  - In spite of what I am feeling, I am capable and can handle this situation.

  - In spite of what I am feeling, I am not alone.

  - In spite of what I am feeling, I am safe in this place.

  - In spite of what I am feeling, this situation is only happening now, not forever. I am not trapped.

- Reflect on the people for whom you have difficulty showing compassion. Consider where this difficulty might be coming from. Is the source of the difficulty inside your own story?

- Who are the voices that have helped you build a strong inner self? What are some of the specific words they have used to describe you?

- Think of a situation when you were a child that is painful or shameful to remember. Write a letter of comfort from your adult self to your child self. Assure your child self that it wasn't their fault and they are safe now.

Discussion questions for staff

- A compassionate work environment is important for our staff, as well as for those we serve. How does our current treatment of each other and those we serve reflect a compassionate organizational culture?

- Regular affirmations can be helpful in building a strong staff identity. At a staff meeting, take a few minutes to exchange words of affirmation. One colleague says to another something like, "John, I really appreciate your kindness when I'm in a bad mood." John is allowed to say only "thank you" in return. A couple minutes of this is worth including at every meeting.

Activities to explore

- When working with people in any setting, using visuals can be an effective way to defuse strong emotions. By directing people's attention to a visual on a piece of paper or a whiteboard, the thinking part of the brain can be engaged with less interference from emotions. Practice using visuals with coworkers, and share with each other ways to use visuals. These can include drawings, charts, photographs, and even simple word lists.

- Under stress, it can be difficult to identify our emotions. Find an easy-to-use list of names of feelings to look at when emotions are high. Reading through the list and deciding which word most specifically describes your current reaction can be helpful in reintegrating your brain.

- Schools often use "brain breaks" to assist students. Brain breaks help your brain reset, defuse stress, and refocus on the next task at hand. Come up with some brain breaks for yourself to use when you recognize increasing stress/anxiety. Examples include:

  - Take a quick walk—outside if possible.

  - Do any physical activity that requires effort, such as walking up a flight of stairs or doing a few jumping jacks, push-ups, or sit-ups.

  - Take a thinking break. For a short time (even just a minute), stop thinking and let your mind drift. Stare out the window or get lost in the motion of your screen saver. Watching a video of a kaleidoscope can be a great thinking break as well.

  - Take a minute to get a glass of water and drink it.

- Look at photos on your phone for a minute—but not photos on social media. Store some photos that are positive and personal to you. They could be nature photos or memories from a family vacation, for example. They should be calming and separate from the other pictures on your phone. Don't just scroll through your phone's camera roll or your best friend's Instagram.

Interlude: Metaphor Story

A Hole in Your Heart

by Rubén Perez

> *"I love this story by Rubén Perez. Where you have a 'hole in your heart' is where your shame is, and it is where you work to fill that hole in your heart."*
>
> —Ruby Payne

During my third year of teaching, I was faced with the dilemma of having to deal with the reality that we had a kleptomaniac loose in our elementary school. I was certain it was not one of my students as I felt I had a good grasp of what occurred in my immediate circle. We were in the middle of the school year when the pattern of missing items gained momentum. It started with one or two missing items a week and progressed to an almost daily occurrence within a month. Pencils, erasers, rulers, and various other personal items were disappearing, slowly at first and then much more rapidly as the year progressed. At some point my students started to accept it as normal, and even more tragically, expected. When we returned from recess or transitional classes, students would do an immediate desk check and announce what was missing. Comments like, "Well, whoever it is got my ruler," "Yeah, my new pencil is missing," and "I don't leave anything in my desk anymore; I take everything with me because I know somebody is going to steal something" were becoming more frequent.

My frustration level over this reality was extremely high. I just could not understand how this person could not be caught in a time period spanning about four weeks. On a day when my students were in music class, the principal called a last-minute meeting for our fifth-grade team. I ran to my classroom to get a folder where I kept notes for every meeting we held. As I walked in, I saw a student of mine named Sammy on his knees, quietly sifting through the contents of a desk in the middle of the classroom. I was so focused on getting my folder that it took me a minute to realize he was not at his assigned desk; he was at someone else's desk. It was at this moment that I stopped and looked at him. He was red-faced and staring back at me. I knew him to be reserved, timid, and sensitive. He was the kind of child whose shy mannerisms could easily make him invisible in a crowd.

"Sammy, it's you?"

He replied "yes" in a whisper and stood there motionless. With purposeful and directive delivery, I asked him to put back everything he had just taken and return to music class, and I informed him we now had an appointment to have lunch together the next day. His shame-filled demeanor led me to believe I had little to worry about between that moment and our scheduled conversation.

It was during our talk that I asked all the typical questions most people would ask: "Why have you been taking other people's property? Weren't you afraid of getting caught? Don't you know that this type of behavior will only lead to worse problems?"

I felt increasingly defeated as Sammy gave answers that didn't help the situation. He kept responding with noncommittal and ill-focused answers that were laced with enough guilt and shame to prevent us from having a meaningful conversation. "I don't know," he would say, or, "Yeah, I know." Despite the shallowness and choppy nature of our conversation, Sammy's nonverbals were communicating something I didn't fully understand. I proceeded with a gut feeling.

"Sammy, is there someone in your life who calls you stupid?" That is when his eyes locked onto mine.

"Yes."

"Who is it?"

"My mom."

I instantly and instinctively regretted asking the question. How in the world could I possibly address Sammy being called stupid by his mother without diminishing her in his eyes? I needed to advocate for Sammy, but I also felt the weight of having to advocate for the relationship he had with his mother.

"I have a question, Sammy. When your mother calls you stupid, is she ever in a good mood? Does she only say that word when she is stressed or angry?"

His facial expression told me that he was deep in thought and trying to be as honest as possible. "She only says it when she's angry."

I said, "I'm not going to defend anyone for calling you stupid. It's wrong and it's hurtful. What I will say is this: The fact that your mother does not call you stupid when she is in a good mood and when things are going well is your proof that she really does love you. I've met your mother, and I know a little bit of what goes on in her life. She has three jobs, and I can only imagine the amount of stress she is under on a daily basis. She is working very hard to keep a home and pay the bills. When people are angry or stressed, they sometimes yell at the people they love the most. I don't know why that is, but it's the people we believe will never run away from us who often get the harshest treatment. It's not that your mother thinks you're stupid. It's that she is so frustrated that she takes her anger out on people at home, away from the people who affect her job. But that part doesn't help you at all. It just hurts regardless of why it happens. By the looks of things, it hurts pretty deeply.

"Do you know what a black hole is?" I asked. We had already established ourselves as huge Star Wars fans, and Sammy was particularly interested in space.

"Of course," he said. "It's a hole in space that has superpower suction. It is so strong it even absorbs light."

"That's correct. It is so strong that it takes in anything around it. When our hearts carry a hurt, it can sometimes feel like our hearts have a black hole. Hearts can get so hurt and so empty that it can make us feel a sense of urgency to fill it with something. Black holes don't care what you fill them with; they are hungry for anything that is close to them.

"Here is what I suspect might be happening, Sammy. When you take things, it feels exciting. Sometimes, there is a little bit of an adrenaline rush when we break rules and try not to get caught. When you take things, the excitement can make it feel like you are putting something in the black hole of your heart."

While I was saying this, I also mimed the actions of grabbing things for visual purposes. I slowly grabbed pencils, markers, tape rolls, etc. and placed them inside my shirt, where I kept them pressed against my heart. The visual caught his attention.

"The problem is that the excitement does not last very long. So, you do it again. Then again and again. Pretty soon, you have a habit of taking things just to feel the excitement. Sammy, a black hole never gets full. You must deal with the reason it exists first. No ruler or pencil will ever fill the hurt."

He was quiet for a while. He affirmed that what I demonstrated was very similar to his experience. We spoke a bit more before I felt it was time to address his actions.

"Sammy, there is a saying that goes: 'Hurt people hurt people.'"

He thought for a minute and replied, "Like my mom sometimes hurts me because she is hurt?"

"Exactly! Now let's talk about how taking people's belongings is a repeat of this cycle."

He immediately recognized the parallel, and there was a strange combination of guilt and relief on his face. I surmised that he finally understood why he did what he did. He didn't want to hurt other people; he was not focused on that part of the equation. After he admitted full responsibility for his actions, he agreed to return all the items he had taken. Two weeks later, Sammy approached me and said that ever since our conversation, he had stopped stealing. More significantly, he had also stopped having the *need* to steal as well. We did not have an issue with missing items for the rest of the school year.

Sammy was not, in any way, shape, or form, a bad kid. He was a hurt kid whose actions hurt others while he was trying to cope with his own pain. I did not excuse his actions, nor did I minimize the offense of theft. My assessment was that Sammy's emotional wound needed attention first. Only then would he be able to take his eyes off himself to see how his actions affected others. It was so gratifying to see him accept full responsibility and start making decisions based on a deeper level of empathy for himself and his classmates.

Chapter Four

How the Workplace Creates Emotional Issues and Impacts the Story You Tell About Yourself

'Less than' and 'separate from' experiences

Many times, what sets an individual off emotionally in the workplace are the nonverbals and biases of the workplace. These nonverbals are often interpreted as "I am less than, or separate from," and they create emotional responses.

About 80% of all communication is nonverbal. As was stated in the first chapter, the autonomic nervous system is an energy system. If you have ever been in a room with an angry person, you could feel their anger. That is because the electromagnetic waves go three feet out from the body. According to the FBI, the most offensive nonverbal signal in the world is eye-rolling.

Furthermore, because the emotional self (the amygdala) is highly structured by the time we are three years old, before we have much language, many of the learned responses that we use are simply at the subconscious level; we act on them even though we don't know why. This leads to implicit bias. In the book *Plays Well with Others: The Surprising Science Behind Why Everything You Know About Relationships Is (Mostly) Wrong*, author Eric Barker states "70% of first impressions are accurate." That means 30% are inaccurate, and "a fair amount of this inaccuracy is due to your biased brain…Numerous studies have found that we have a bias against noticing our biases." Barker goes on to talk about cognitive biases, and the main issue with those is confirmation bias. In other words, we look for examples to reinforce what we already believe. As Barker states, "first impressions are fairly accurate. But once they are set, they're extremely hard to change."[34]

Right now, implicit bias is often used to examine racial bias, but it is much broader than that, as this chart examines.

It is important to note that bias is always a two-way street and impacts nonverbals and communication.

Area of bias	Bias for	Bias against	No judgment
Eyes (look at you, look away, etc.)			
Educational attainment level/ vocabulary			
Race (same as you, not a member of the dominant race/culture/ethnicity/ country of origin/religion, etc.)			
Gender			
Appearance (cleanliness, smell, hair)			
Body tells (anxious, comfortable)			
Emotional status (fear, anger, joy)			
Energy (lethargic, high energy)			
Weight			
Age			
Ability or disability			
Physical fitness			
Occupation			
Shoes/boots			
Clothes/jewelry			
Dialect/speech/language			

Many of these biases impact personal interactions and became "understandings" before we had vocabulary. Often, a person is rejected on the basis of biases that are subtle and unnamed. If a person has enough of those experiences of "less than and separate from," then it begins to create a weaker inner self as opposed to a stronger inner self.

If these "less than and separate from" issues are deep enough, they create wounds. Wounds can come in the form of trauma, adverse childhood experiences, negligence, abuse, addiction, etc.

These experiences can come from racism, sexism, disability, age, immigration, socioeconomic class, etc.

Dominant culture and racial and gender discrimination

Dominant culture is defined by Oxford Reference in the following way:

> Whereas traditional societies can be characterized by a high consistency of cultural traits and customs, modern societies are often a conglomeration of different, often competing, cultures and subcultures. In such a situation of diversity, a dominant culture is one whose values, language, and ways of behaving are imposed on a subordinate culture or cultures through economic or political power. This may be achieved through legal or political suppression of other sets of values and patterns of behavior, or by monopolizing the media of communication.[35]

Depending on where you are in the world, the dominant culture can vary. In India, it is the top two castes. In China, it is people of Han descent.

In the U.S., two of the key issues in the workplace are racial and gender discrimination. "In 2020, women earned 83 cents to every dollar earned by men."[36]

When it comes to the racial wage gap,

> differences that emerge are taken as evidence of racial discrimination. Research has found wage and employment discrimination against Blacks, Native Americans, Hispanics, and Asians; however, discrimination has been found to be a much larger contributing factor for Black wages than wages of other races.

> A study conducted by Grodsky & Pager found that individual attributes, such as human capital and region, account for just more than half of the Black–White wage gap, and an additional 20 percent is due to different occupational distributions between Blacks and Whites. The remaining portion of the wage gap not accounted for by individual and occupational distribution factors is thought to be due, at least in part, to discrimination.

> Discrimination based on race has been found in other research as well. Seventy-four percent of employers in one study were found to be racially biased against Blacks, and Blacks have been found to make lower wages than Whites working in the same industry. White Latinos earn higher wages than non-White Latinos, regardless of whether they are native or immigrant, suggesting possible discrimination based on skin color. Additionally, many employers openly admit to discriminating against

Blacks and workers in the inner city, as one study by Kirschenman and Neckerman found. Hiring audits have also found discrimination in the labor market. Based on data from the 1990s to 2003, when Black and White applicants hold the same credentials, Whites receive jobs at a rate of 3:1.[37]

Any way in which the dominant culture makes an individual or group of people feel "less than" or "separate from" can increase shame, guilt, and humiliation.

What develops shame, guilt, and humiliation?

When the adults do not provide predictable safety and belonging, then the child usually concludes that there is something wrong with the child (anxiety), dismisses the attachment to the adult (avoidance), or becomes fragmented and distorted (safe and dangerous). All of these are sources of shame because the child has to choose an attachment for survival. As a result, the child cannot see the adult as faulty but rather sees the self as faulty. Children in these situations assume that they are "less than" and "separate from" the adult and others.

The neurobiology of shame

Because the majority of brain development in the first two years of life is in the right side of the brain (which deals with feelings, movement, sensory data, etc.), and because language is not developed yet, the information becomes *embodied.* It becomes a "felt experience" and impacts the sympathetic nervous system. The response is immediate and without thought. Our blood sugar goes up, our eyes lower, we have a heaviness in our chest, and we "feel bad." Because emotions are 200 to 5,000 times faster than thought, it is a *felt* experience and we cannot name it. In this process, the prefrontal cortex becomes disengaged and fragmented and our first instinct is to be alone—away from the feeling.

Shame is learned between the ages of 18 and 24 months[38] and is almost always triggered by a nonverbal that indicates you are less than and separate from. Shame always occurs in the context of a relationship and almost always involves a shift of emotional state. It often happens when we are relaxed and happy and all of a sudden something happens, the shift is so fast, we feel bad, and we want to leave or attack.

Shame works to modify behavior if a person has belonging, because they do not want to lose their relationships (tribe, family, clan, group, etc.). But shame *does not* work if a person does not have belonging. In that case, shame increases social isolation, aggression, and rage.

Shame is as much, if not more, about the person who does the shaming than the person being shamed. Unrecognized shame often becomes a lie we believe about ourselves. And in our brains, we create a "shame attendant" who voices this to us on a frequent basis. It is important for the person to recognize this internal voice and refute it by saying: "That is not about me."

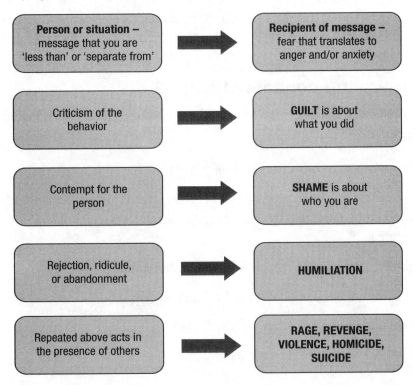

When the inner self is weak and the end result is violence, this may be the progression from 'less than' and 'separate from' to avoidable incidents.

Person or situation – message that you are 'less than' or 'separate from'	**Recipient of message –** fear that translates to anger and/or anxiety
Criticism of the behavior	**GUILT** is about what you did
Contempt for the person	**SHAME** is about who you are
Rejection, ridicule, or abandonment	**HUMILIATION**
Repeated above acts in the presence of others	**RAGE, REVENGE, VIOLENCE, HOMICIDE, SUICIDE**

What are factors that may increase shame? That make individuals feel 'less than' or 'separate from'?

Shame occurs as a result of feeling less than or separate from the majority of the group. During adolescence and throughout adulthood, the driving question is: "How do others see me?" When people feel or are told that others see them as uninteresting, less than, or separate from, a sense of shame may develop.

When the inner self is weak and the end result is violence, this may be the progression from "less than" and "separate from" to avoidable incidents. John Gottman, in his research on marriages and divorce, can predict with 95% accuracy whether a marriage will end in divorce. He outlines a process that progresses in this manner: conflict, then criticism, then contempt, then silence (I don't talk to you and you don't talk to me, or we are not in the same space together), then separation. He says when four out of five interactions are negative, the couple divorces.

Anger

What causes anger?

According to Bowlby, anger is based upon fear and is a response to separation, grief, and loss.[39]

What are the benefits of anger?

Stosny indicates that anger has benefits for the person who is angry, including:

1. It is an analgesic (numbs the pain).

2. It is an amphetamine (provides energy).

3. It allows one to seize power "by energizing behavior, advertising potency and determination, and by overriding feelings of anxiety, vulnerability, and ego threat."[40]

4. It protects the inner self from suffering further harm.

5. It provides moral justification and validation.

6. It provides temporary relief from self-ache.

7. It provides a way to deal with fear.

Why does the brain go to the negative first?

1. Negative emotions produce greater effects. Survival often requires immediate response. Anger, fear, disgust, and distress are often related to survival.

2. Loss is always more powerful and stays in memory longer than gain. If you win $1,000, you are happy. If you lose $1,000, you remember it for a long time.

3. "Signal retreat" keeps our emotions from overwhelming us. Signal retreat means that emotions become weaker over time. It is not possible to hold on to the intensity of an emotion that is always occurring. Over time that feeling becomes the norm.

Why does the intensity of the feeling matter?

Often the intensity is related to self-validation. Intensity can occur when the brain goes straight from possibility to probability. *I know I am right even if I am wrong!*

According to Stosny, individuals can become addicted to anger. If you are dealing with a person who is addicted to anger, often the anger is used as a buffer to keep from experiencing further damage to the inner self. Abusive spouses

> convert feelings of vulnerability into anger and rage, blaming their shame and vulnerability on their attachment figures, against whose perceived assaults they feel compelled to defend themselves...Anger used in this way—as a mechanism of externalization—serves an important protective function, guarding an already bruised or damaged or defective self from further assault of guilt, shame, and abandonment/engulfment anxiety.[41]

Anxiety

Anxiety is about fear, uncertainty, and discomfort.

When people are anxious, they are engaging in "what if" thinking. Uncertainty and discomfort occur when there is worry about safety, belonging, and acceptance. Anxious parents tend to produce anxious children.[42]

Avoidance

Avoidance is a behavioral attempt to deal with a negative emotion. It is often related to rejection and is an attack emotion. When you have coworkers who avoid work, they often have no hope, interest, or joy in the people around them. There often is not any value seen in working because it is not related to an emotional payoff. It may even require interacting with another human being who is seen as having little value.

Shame, humiliation, guilt

These three words—*shame*, *humiliation*, and *guilt*—are often used interchangeably and without clarity.

Shame is about identity, about who you are.

Humiliation occurs when criticism or contempt is added to shame.

Guilt is about something you have done.

Shame occurs when you are found to be uninteresting, unattractive, less than, separate from. One of the societal issues that happens if a person is a member of a marginalized group is that the dominant culture will make distinctions and separations based on the differences as opposed to focusing on the similarities.

Shame is very difficult, if not impossible, to address unless the person experiencing shame can name the specific reality that is happening.

Shame: You are a fraud—someone is going to find out.

Humiliation occurs when criticism or contempt is added to the shame, e.g., "You are not good because you are..." Criticism is about the behavior. Contempt is about the person. If the contempt or criticism comes when you are young or in your adolescence, then your inner self may be weak. If there is no adult who is compassionate to you and cares about you, then your inner self may become the motivation for undesirable behaviors.

Guilt is about something you do for which you can ask forgiveness.

Violence in the workplace

These numbers from the U.S. Bureau of Justice Statistics show that while workplace murders have declined since the 1990s, violent crime in the workplace still occurs at a high rate.

Workplace homicide, 1992–2019

- A total of 17,865 workers were victims of workplace homicides from 1992 to 2019.

- A total of 454 workplace homicides took place in 2019, which marked a 58% decrease from a peak of 1,080 recorded in 1994.

Nonfatal workplace violence, 2015–2019

- The average annual rate of nonfatal workplace violence was eight violent crimes per 1,000 workers age 16 or older.

- On average, 1.3 million nonfatal violent crimes in the workplace occurred annually.[43]

Domestic violence in the workplace

Domestic violence takes a physical and emotional toll on survivors, most of whom are women—and it has an economic impact as well.

> One in every four women and one in 10 men will experience domestic violence in their lifetime, according to the Centers for Disease Control and Prevention (CDC). The Department of Labor reports that victims of domestic violence lose nearly 8 million days of paid work per year in the U.S., resulting in a $1.8 billion loss in productivity for employers... The CDC also reported that an estimated 1.3 million women are victims of physical assault by an intimate partner each year and that 85 percent of domestic violence victims are women.[44]

Rage, revenge, and violence

Rage often comes out of contempt. Violence comes from too little compassion.

> *The problem of violence is less a matter of too much of something* (e.g., anger, aggression, exertion of power and control, negative attitudes toward women and children) *than of too little of something, namely compassion, moral judgment, and relationship skills*...Research indicates that merely changing situational behavior runs the risk of increasing physical abuse...or increasing psychological abuse even as physical abuse wanes...Social attitudes are the most superficial facet of an individual's belief system. They reflect self-constructions while having no causal effect on them. As such they serve merely as excuses.[45]

According to Salman Akhtar and Henri Parens, editors of the book *Revenge: Narcissistic Injury, Rage, and Retaliation,* revenge involves rage, envy, and resentment.

> An injury that has been repaid, even if only in words, is recollected quite differently from one that has to be accepted...an injury that has been suffered in silence as "a mortification"...The injured person's reaction to the trauma only exercises a completely "cathartic" effect if it is an adequate reaction—as, for instance, revenge.[46]

Akhtar and Parens go on to say that using language to explore the damage rather than taking an action is almost as effective.

In the research, compassion, kindness, gratitude, and reparation act as counterbalances to malignant narcissism and revenge. However, the researchers note that often individuals who have envy and malignant narcissism hate goodness, kindness, and support. The reason is that without the anger and rage, the self-soothing that occurs is absent, and the weak inner self is not soothed.

Every person has wounds

The question is whether your wounds define you or become just another part of your self. If they define you, your growth stagnates. If they become a part of you, your growth accelerates. If you have ever met someone who got a divorce 20 years ago and is still bitter and angry, you have met someone who has defined their life by a wound.

The authors have met individuals who have been so wounded by an issue or person or event that it defines them for the rest of their life. It may have been a death, divorce, an injury based on racial or gender identity, an illness, etc.

"Disruption is when narrative is most useful. When something unexpectedly happens, something challenging, we need a story."[47]

Here are nine of the most common kinds of wounds. The possible cause of the behavior is also identified.[48] This is adapted from work on the Enneagram.

Childhood experience/ message/story/wound	May cause this emotion and behavior	What they want from people in power
1. Environment emphasized that one must be good and correct. Do not make mistakes. The world is black and white—right or wrong. Competition to be the best.	Anger at self. Want to be perfect. Resent those who do not follow the rules.	Neatness and order. All the details. Clarify the criteria. Establish that perfection is not necessarily the goal.
2. Environment taught them that having or expressing their own needs leads to humiliation or rejection. Work to adapt to the needs of others in their environment.	Driven by feelings/heart. Focus on others' feelings rather than their own.	Help them limit what they say yes to doing. Have them identify their own feelings. Help them identify what they need in a situation.

(continued on next page)

(continued from previous page)

Childhood experience/ message/story/wound	May cause this emotion and behavior	What they want from people in power
3. Environment where they were valued and rewarded for getting things done. Don't believe that they can be loved if they are not productive. Child may take on parenting roles.	Ignore feelings—focus on tasks.	Opportunities for leadership. Identify the end result, and let them do the work. Ask them to identify what they sacrifice in their pursuit of achievement. What has value in their life aside from achievement?
4. Early environment in which they felt different and misunderstood by their parents, siblings, and peers. Lots of "what if?" Feel as if something is always missing.	Focus on their own feelings. They are their feelings.	Want to be recognized as unique and different. Want to be creative. Identify realistic situations as opposed to idealistic situations.
5. Often felt invisible as a child. Grew up either with an intrusive parent or a lack of deep, meaningful interactions with caregivers. Retreat to the world of thoughts. To survive, need to detach emotionally and hide.	Fear is outside of them. Focus on facts/information and research.	Understand their need for solitude, exploration of the unknown, undiscovered. Want time for their projects. Do not want to feel uninformed or ignorant, to be "managed." Value autonomy and self-containment.
6. Often, not always, something unpredictable about early childhood environment. Learned there is always something to worry about.	Fear is internal. I am afraid for me.	Want to have security, belonging, predictability. Want to eliminate threats as much as possible.
7. In developmental years, the message was: "You're on your own. Little support here." Create their own nirvana.	Ignore fear. Trade fear for experiences—the next adventure.	Want to maintain freedom and happiness, experience lots of variety, be excited and occupied, and avoid pain. Do not want to feel trapped, bored, or guilty.

(continued on next page)

(continued from previous page)

Childhood experience/ message/story/wound	May cause this emotion and behavior	What they want from people in power
8. Loss of childhood innocence or other experience that required them to take responsibility for self and others. Unstable environments or backgrounds where toughness was rewarded, or bullied at school.	Direct anger at others. Arguing is intimacy and connection. Intense energy—all or nothing. Do not try to control me.	Challenge them right back. Tell them the truth—don't sugarcoat it. Let them have some sort of control over the situation—offer choices. Appeal to their soft side.
9. Grew up in environments where they felt unimportant and that their opinions and wants did not matter much.	Deny their anger. Try to get everyone to get along. Tune out and withdraw to a safe place.	Enjoy structure, predictability, routines. Like to be part of a group with good relationships. Don't want conflict or stress.

Your wounds become a part of your story of who you are.

Where do you get the story of who you are?

Your memory and the stories you carry in your head—identity.

"My experiences trump your truth."
–Dr. Rickey Frierson

"The universe is made up of stories, not of atoms."
–Muriel Rukeyser [49]

The hippocampus

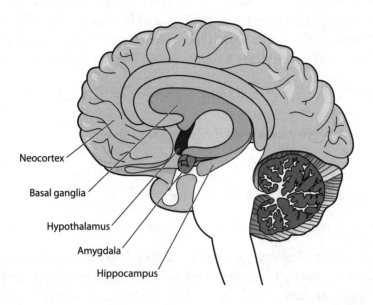

Neocortex

Basal ganglia

Hypothalamus

Amygdala

Hippocampus

The hippocampus is the part of the brain where we keep our memories and stories of who we are.

Scientists have long known that recording a memory requires adjusting the connections between neurons. Each memory tweaks some tiny subset of the neurons in the brain (the human brain has 100 billion neurons in all), changing the way they communicate. Neurons send messages to one another across narrow gaps called synapses. A synapse is like a bustling port, complete with machinery for sending and receiving cargo—neurotransmitters, specialized chemicals that convey signals between neurons. All of the shipping machinery is built from proteins, the basic building blocks of cells…Eric Kandel [is] a neuroscientist at Columbia University in New York City. In five decades of research, Kandel has shown how short-term memories—those lasting a few minutes—involve relatively quick and simple chemical changes to the synapse that make it work more efficiently. Kandel, who won a share of the 2000 Nobel Prize in Physiology or Medicine, found that to build a memory that lasts hours, days, or years, neurons must manufacture new proteins and expand the docks, as it were, to make the neurotransmitter traffic run more efficiently. Long-term memories must literally be built into the brain's synapses.[50]

From these long-term memories, we in part construct the "story" of who we are. Early childhood and adolescent experiences create internal stories and responses. As a group of researchers led by Kate McLean at Western Washington University states, "The stories we tell about ourselves reveal ourselves, construct ourselves, and sustain ourselves through time."[51] We act on those stories.

As McLean states, the following aspects of these long-term memories contribute to our story:

1. Identity development is a crucial psychosocial task.

2. Identity is constructed, it does not simply arise.

3. Identity is constructed through narrative.

4. And most importantly…identity is not constructed alone.[52]

Just as there are the "big five" personality traits that are universal (neuroticism/less neurotic, openness to experience/less open to experience, extraversion/introversion, agreeableness/less agreeable, and conscientious/less conscientious), there is growing awareness that there are the "big three" key features of internal stories. These big three are:

1. **Motivational and affective themes:** (a) How much autonomy and connection is there? (b) What is the ratio of positive to negative stories? (c) Are the stories dominated by good situations turning bad or bad situations working out well in the end?

2. **Autobiographical reasoning:** (a) How much do we think about our stories? (b) Can we extrapolate meaning? (c) Can we see links between key events? (d) Can we identify ways in which we have and have not changed?

3. **Structure:** How much do our stories make sense, and are they coherent in terms of the timeline, the context, and the facts?

People who have no connection between the past and the now, no sense of the future—e.g., who they were, who they are, and who they will be—are associated in the research with suicidal ideation and are prone to alcoholism, violent youth offenses, depression, and mental illness. "In fact, many of the conflicts in the world, from simple road rage to outright war, can be seen as stemming from fractured identities."[53]

With the loss of the immediate and extended family and religious and cultural traditions, the questioning of authority and adults, travel, moving, and lack of stable neighborhoods, and with so many outside sources influencing identity formation (media), maintaining a coherent sense of self is very difficult. "The existential angst that comes from the emptiness, meaninglessness, disconnection, and fluidity of modern society creates a need for 'identity work.'"[54]

Psychotherapy, consumerism, and the distraction of entertainment have attempted to fill that need, but they have not been very effective, and in some cases have made things worse.

"Narrative ecology of self" refers to a compilation of stories that a person hears and sees (and sometimes is not told), the stories others tell of that person, and the social context of the stories.

This is McLean's model of narrative ecology of self.[55]

Identity is held in the stories we tell ourselves about ourselves, in the stories others tell about us, and in the stories our culture tells.

Betrayals

Many wounds come in the form of a betrayal.

It is important to remember that betrayals are never about you. They are about the person who did them and that person's driving emotional force to address an injury/need that they have.

Examples of betrayals are legendary in literature, in religion, in history. They are part of the human condition. From Shakespeare's portrayal of betrayal in *Julius Caesar* ("Et tu, Brute?") to the betrayal of Jesus by Judas for 30 pieces of silver to the betrayal of the German people by Hitler, almost all betrayals are about the person doing the betraying. But in the limbic system, a betrayal is portrayed as "there is something wrong with me."

One of the most intense betrayals is death. It is such a loss. And if loss of a parent occurs for an adolescent—particularly between the ages of 12 and 15—the emotional intensity is life-altering.

Strategy: Swapping a toxic coauthor with a healthy coauthor

Key parts of anyone's stories are who they identify as "coauthors." Coauthors can be toxic or healthy, but either way, they help you write the story of who you are. Coauthors are individuals who are in our lives and who help us shape the stories of ourselves.[56]

There is a technique you can use with a person when they tell you that they can't do something. In this technique, you have an individual recall an incident that was negative. You ask them who was present when that happened. What were the comments that were made? Then you ask them for the name of someone who was very supportive of them. Ask them to switch out the "negative" coauthor with the "positive, supportive" coauthor. Then you replay the scenario with the comments from the positive coauthor.

I, Ruby, have a friend who had a very negative parent. This parent constantly berated him, particularly in middle and high school. I asked him if he had had an adult in high school who liked him. He said yes, so I asked him to replay a scenario he remembered with the positive adult rather than the negative one. What would the positive person say? He was amazed. Basically, this exercise can allow the negative memory to be significantly reduced. It helps a person understand that any situation can be played out several different ways depending on the coauthor who is present.

"The present rearranges the past. We never tell the story whole because a life isn't a story; it's a Milky Way of events, and we are forever picking out constellations from it to fit who and where we are."[57]

How to apply this information in your workplace

Questions to ask yourself about yourself:

1. If you met someone new for the first time, what story would you tell them about yourself?

2. What is a story your mother (caregiver, grandmother, father) tells about you?

3. Can you tell me about something that happened to you in grades K–3? In grades 4–8? In high school?

4. Who is a person you have known your entire life and who knows you? Do you care about them?

5. How much freedom do you have to make your own choices? Use a scale of 1 (never) to 10 (always).

6. When you think about your life, do you have more happy stories or more sad stories?

7. Have you had bad things in your life turn out for the best?

8. How are you the same as you were five years ago? How are you different?

9. Did anything that happened in elementary school help you with high school?

10. What is something you will remember forever?

11. In what ways are you different than the movies and social media like TikTok and Instagram say you should be?

12. Who at work has helped you coauthor who you are at work?

13. Who have you helped coauthor?

14. What biases do you have when you are interviewing someone?

15. Do you feel safe from violence at work? Is there someone who makes you uneasy?

What these questions mean

Question 1: Identifies basic parts of identity. What do they identify as important to know?

Question 2: Stories other people tell about us—particularly our caregiver—are crucial in forming identity.

Question 3: Does their story make sense over time?

Question 4: How solid are their connections and belonging over time?

Question 5: Autonomy is key in allowing someone to determine identity.

Question 6: The ratio of good to bad stories forms identity.

Question 7: Can you take a "bad" event and make it into something good? This is critical for integration and personal growth.

Question 8: Coherence and continuity over time.

Question 9: Integration of past into present.

Question 10: Defining moment. Usually a disruption and crisis point. Almost always motivates change.

Question 11: Can you integrate culturally and have a sense of who you are?

Question 12: Identifies your mentors and collaborators.

Question 13: Identifies mentees and indicates impact at work.

Question 14: These are areas to work on.

Question 15: Talk to someone in the human resources department if you feel unsafe.

Journaling questions and prompts

- Implicit bias is a result of our brains developing patterns for safety, often when we are very young, based on experiences and things we observed in the people with whom we lived. Reflect on the bias chart shared earlier, and write about the implicit biases you have noted in yourself. These may include items in the chart but may also be reflected in attitudes toward whole groups of people based on race, ethnicity, language, etc. By writing about implicit bias, we are more likely to be able to recognize and counteract its impact on our choices and our treatment of others.

- Write about the biases that are hard for you to overcome. It is much better to admit we have biases than to tell ourselves and others that we don't. Implicit bias is human. By making bias explicit (i.e., by being conscious of it and acknowledging its influence on our reactions and behaviors), we can develop intentional ways of not allowing bias to impact the service we provide at work.

- Write about times and situations in which you have felt "less than" or "separate from." If they are from your past, how have those experiences impacted your present life in terms of your sense of self and your comfort in various environments?

Discussion questions for staff

- Implicit bias in the workplace is often about hidden rules that manifest as unspoken expectations we have for each other and for those we serve. Often, this becomes the "common sense" we assume people should have. Discuss expectations for staff and for clients/customers.

  - What hidden rules do we have?

  - What happens when someone breaks those rules?

  - Which populations have the most difficulty accessing our services?

  - How are we breaking down barriers to access that arise when our organization assumes clients/customers share our "common sense"?

- Implicit bias within a system is often an issue of first impressions. Conduct an honest examination of what it is like for someone to access our services for the first time. Do we have expectations that create a "less than and separate from" experience before we have even started? How can we improve our first interaction with clients/customers?

- Not everyone in the office has the same biases, nor do we all act on each bias in the same way. Is there a process for colleagues to pass clients/customers to each other in order to better match personalities and interaction styles?

Activities to explore

- The Enneagram can be a useful tool for understanding ourselves and others. Rather than looking at characteristics of people, it looks more deeply at the inner hurts and motivations that result in different strategies for showing up in life and getting our needs met. Consider studying this yourself, or perhaps use it as a staff activity. There are business-oriented applications of the material that can have a positive effect on staff communication.

- The physical space we work in can have an impact on our emotions. If you have physical space, such as a desk or a part of an office or a cubicle, consider adding physical cues (pictures, objects, notes with important sayings, etc.) that you can use to anchor yourself when you are stressed.

- Pick a characteristic you want to focus on for a period of time—perhaps a day or a week. This can be represented by a word or a phrase, e.g., *kindness*, or "How are my reactions reflecting kindness?" Doing this with a trusted coworker can allow you to debrief your experiences together.

Chapter Five

Stages of Adult Development

Age and stages of adult development

Yet another factor in the emotional noise in the workplace is where coworkers are in terms of their own adult development. Sometimes you have two colleagues who are at very different stages of development, as the following story illustrates.

A story: Simply devastated

A friend of mine was working with a high school English department. One of the teachers was a beginning teacher in her 20s. Another teacher in the department was a veteran teacher in her mid-40s. They got into an argument, and the teacher in her 20s started crying.

She said to the older teacher, "You are no friend of mine. You should not think or say that!"

The veteran teacher patted her heart melodramatically and said, "Oh, that tugs at my heartstrings. I am simply devastated!" And then the veteran teacher laughed.

Two very different stages of adult development! In the research, adults in their 20s are very concerned with what you "should" do to be an adult. By the time you are in your mid-40s, you have had a wealth of experience, and you know that not everyone is

Adults, like children, go through different stages of development as they age.

going to be your friend or agree with you. Experience becomes a huge factor in your decisions.

The emotional noise in that particular English department was quite high. The teachers in that department had difficulty working together for several reasons. One of the reasons was that the teachers were at very different stages and facing very different adult development tasks.

Gail Sheehy, in her book *Passages: Predictable Crises of Adult Life*, discusses how she has identified some of these issues in her research with adults.

To remember:

1. These stages are not prescriptive but descriptive.

2. These stages represent patterns that individuals at that age tend to have. Not everyone will experience that age in that way.

3. "During each of these…[stages], how we feel about our way of living will undergo subtle changes in four areas of perception. One is the interior sense of self in relation to others. A second is the proportion of safeness to danger we feel in our lives. A third is our perception of time—do we have plenty of it, or are we beginning to feel that time is running out? Last, there will be some shift at the gut level in our sense of aliveness or stagnation."[58]

4. "Times of crisis, of disruption or constructive change, are not only predictable but desirable. They mean growth."[59]

5. A person may need to experience a crisis before identity can be fully developed.

6. According to behavioral theorists, both boys and girls have their primary attachment to the mother.

7. "When the tasks of one period remain largely unmet, they will complicate or interfere with the work on the tasks of the next period. In the extreme case, development may be impaired to such a degree that the person cannot truly enter the new period."[60]

The stagnation and staying alive issue is huge. Everyone knows an adult who is angry and bitter. Almost everyone knows someone who got divorced 20 years ago but acts as if it happened yesterday. *Every human being has wounds.*

Do you allow your wounds to heal, or are they constantly bleeding and you have to attend to them every day? If you let them heal, you may have a scar. If you cannot let them heal, then your wounds significantly impact the last part of your life. The research is that your physical health is also impacted if you become stagnant.

Basic adult development tasks

Regardless of race, country of origin, birth order, etc., these are developmental tasks that every adult faces:

Identity – Who am I?

Intimacy – Who am I in relationship to another?

Independence/autonomy – What can I do on my own?

Purpose/meaning – Why am I alive?

Work/role – What value do I bring?

Limitations of time – What do I do with the time I have?

Aging/death – How do I deal with the aging and death of others? How do I deal with my own aging and end-of-life issues?

All of these adult development tasks create emotional responses. Every individual has a choice to ignore or delay the development, but the issue will keep returning to be addressed.

Age frame	Tasks/issues/key questions
18–22 'Pulling up roots'	**Key question: What am I going to do with my life?** Four tasks: Find a peer-group role, a sex role, an occupation, and a worldview/set of beliefs. Establish autonomy and identity. De-idealize the parent or parent substitute in order to start trusting own judgment. Big focus on what you do not want to do or be. In 2017, 30% of individuals under the age of 30 lived at home with their parents. These developmental tasks occur even if the individual is living at home. They may be delayed, but the issues of identity, intimacy, occupation, and a worldview/set of beliefs tend to develop.

(continued on next page)

(continued from previous page)

Age frame	Tasks/issues/key questions
22–28 'Trying 20s'	**Key question: What should I do to be an adult?** Tasks: Shape a dream, prepare for life's work, find a mentor, develop intimacy with another. Have a deep fear that choices are irrevocable. Strong belief that I will never be like my parents, that partners will grow together at equal speeds. A time of competing forces—stability and structure versus exploration and experimentation. Reasons for marriage in the 20s include: the need for safety, the need to fill some vacancy in yourself, the need to get away from home, the need for prestige or practicality.[61] The presence or absence of a mentor at this time "has enormous impact on development…The lack of mentors…is a great developmental handicap."[62] There is a tendency to marry someone who has many characteristics of or plays a similar role to one of our parents.
28–32 'Passage to the 30s'	**Key question: Do I agree with the adult that I am becoming?** Tasks: Revisit the decisions involving identity, intimacy, independence, marriage (lots of first divorces occur at this time), children (to have or not to have), career choices (do I really want to do this?), etc. Strong belief that there is still time to do it all. Women see it as a last chance in terms of children, career, and life path. Men often press the accelerator harder. Marriage satisfaction decreases. "For the past 50 years, Americans have been most likely to break out of wedlock when the man is about 30 and the woman is about 28."[63] Learns that intelligence is not as well rewarded as loyalty. Learns that not all difficulties can be solved with willpower and intellect.

(continued on next page)

(continued from previous page)

Age frame	Tasks/issues/key questions
32–39 'Settling down'	**Key question: How do I achieve balance?** Tasks: "To sort out the qualities we want to retain from our childhood models, to blend them with the qualities and capacities that distinguish us as individuals, and to fit all this back together in some broader form."[64] Women come "to understand that it is probably not possible for a woman to work out a combination of the two careers (domestic and extra-familial) until 30 or 35."[65] Conflict between safety and autonomy, freedom and stability. Time is a huge issue—there is not enough. Squeezed between demands of children, career, aging parents, family dynamics. Strong defense of current beliefs. Fairly certain that their understanding/worldview is correct.
35–45 'Authenticity crisis' 'Danger and opportunity' 'The adolescence of adulthood'	**Key questions: Why am I doing this? What do I really believe?** Tasks: Aliveness versus stagnation. Shift in the sense of time—health, career, mortality (will not live forever). Changes happening in self and in others. New wrinkles appear every day. Taking apart the dream and its illusions to spark renewal. Hormonal changes: Males start producing less testosterone, which allows estrogen to play more of a role (become more nurturing). Females produce less estrogen, and testosterone plays more of a role (become more assertive). "The loss of youth, the faltering of physical powers we have always taken for granted, the fading purpose of stereotyped roles by which we have thus far identified ourselves, the spiritual dilemma of having no absolute answers—any or all of these shocks can throw us into crisis."[66] "Every loose end not resolved in previous passages will resurface to haunt us. These demons may lead us into private hells of depression, sexual promiscuity, power chasing, hypochondria, self-destructive acts (alcoholism, drug taking, car accidents, suicide), and violent swings of mood. All are well documented as rising during the middle years."[67] Must do some grieving for the old self. We do a gut-level reintegration of self, and we face up to our own inevitable death. "37–42 are the peak years of anxiety for almost everyone."[68]

(continued on next page)

(continued from previous page)

Age frame	Tasks/issues/key questions
42–55 'Renewal or resignation'	**Key question: What must I do?** Tasks: Experience becomes a major tool with which decisions are made. Freedom to be independent, one's own self, within a relationship. No one can totally understand who I am. Parents are forgiven. Children are "released" to be adults. Dealing with aging. Key understanding that there is not enough time anymore, so what are my priorities for the time I have left? Motto of this stage is "no more bulls--t."[69] For men, "the 40s are a time for discovering the emotive parts of themselves that didn't fit with the posture of the strong, dynamic, rational young men they were supposed to be at 25."[70] Remember that "middle-aged men and women are the 'norm-bearers and decision-makers,' and that while 'they live in a society…oriented toward youth,' it is 'controlled by the middle-aged'…After 45, most people who have allowed themselves the authenticity crisis are ready to accept entry to middle age and to enjoy its many prerogatives."[71] "The crux of it is to see, to feel, and finally to know that none of us can aspire to fulfillment through someone else."[72]
55–70 and beyond 'Integrity… despair and disgust'	**Key questions: What is my legacy? What am I going to do next? How can I give back?** Tasks: Address career questions. Do I retire or do I stay? If I am forced out of my career, what do I do? If I retire, what will I do next? Health issues. Financial issues: Can I afford to retire? What did/does my life mean? Family commitments and issues—raising grandchildren, etc. More time is devoted to health issues—maintenance, repair, serious illness, etc. According to insurance actuaries, more than one third of individuals who retire are deceased within 18 months.[73] Important to develop new friends—particularly those younger than you. Friends you have had for a long time die. Erikson identifies this time as one of gathering greater authenticity for the life lived versus seeing one's life as a mistake, a waste of time, without meaning or purpose. Integrity makes the 70s one of the happiest times for many adults, while others may become trapped in despair and disgust.

"Everyone has difficulty with the steps of inner growth, even when the outer obstacles appear easily surmountable. What's more, the prizes of our society are reserved for outer, not inner, achievements. Scant are the trophies given for reconciling all the forces that compete to direct our development, although working toward such a reconciliation hour by demanding hour, day by triumphant day, year by exacting year is what underlies all growth of the personality. A great deal of behavioral red tape can be cut through once people have developed judgment enriched by both inner and outer experience. It is this striking improvement in the exercise of judgment."[74]

Importance of mentoring

In the research, if a person does not have a mentor in the workplace in their 20s, it is a developmental handicap for the rest of their career. Many young adults in their 20s believe that a mentor will find them or be assigned to them at work, but that is not how it usually happens. In the research on mentoring youth, the mentor is the key factor in how well the mentoring relationship develops. But in the research on mentoring adults, it is the *mentee* who determines the quality of the mentoring relationship.

Young adults need to find their own mentors. This is the way to do that: (a) Find an adult who does something well in which you are interested, (b) ask that adult if you can meet with them and ask a couple of questions, and (c) based on the quality of that interaction, you then ask them if you can try some of their ideas and meet with them again and talk to them. In that process, the mentor begins to introduce you to other people who know more than they do, and it widens the bridging social capital that the mentee has.

Knowledge versus wisdom

Why would you want a mentor anyway? When a person is in their 20s and 30s, they have a great deal of knowledge and spend time acquiring it. By the time a person is in their 40s—if they have not stagnated and gotten bitter—they have begun to acquire wisdom. Wisdom is the ability to make good decisions with the tacit knowledge base of unspoken understandings. It is the understandings of the interplay of patterns, personalities, situations, legalities, practices, and idiosyncrasies of a situation/profession/quagmire. It is invaluable and is often conveyed through stories.

A mentor can give you those understandings. They are very difficult to find elsewhere.

Generational characteristics

A lot has been written about the characteristics of baby boomers, Generation X, millennials, Generation Z, and Generation Alpha. Scholars and critics examine the cultural influences of each generation and the attributes its members share. Each generation has defining moments. Defining moments for baby boomers were the assassinations of John F. Kennedy and Martin Luther King Jr. and the success of the Apollo 11 moon landing.

This table identifies the generations:

Generation Alpha	2013–2024
Generation Z	1997–2012
Generation Y (millennials)	1981–1996
Generation X	1965–1980
Baby boomers	1946–1964
Silent Generation	1928–1945

Please note that the date ranges are approximate and depend on the researcher.

Each generation comes with its own defining moments, reactions to the subsequent generation, and shared experiences/understandings. There is also diversity within the generations.[75]

How to apply this information in your workplace

1. Where are you in your own developmental stages? How does that impact how you negotiate your workplace?

2. Do you have biases for or against a certain generational age group?

Journaling questions and prompts

- Journal in response to the questions posed by the basic adult development tasks described in Chapter Five. How are your answers different than they might have been 10 years ago (even if you were a kid then)? How might they change as you grow older?

- Write about the best parts of being the age you are. What are the greatest challenges for you at this age?

- Start journaling a list titled "What I Have Learned in Life."

Discussion questions for staff

- If time permits, allow different age groups to give their specific impressions and thoughts about a topic. In a discussion about first impressions and how people are greeted, ask for responses from people in their 20s, 30s, 40s, and so on. This allows differing perspectives to be heard and respected. Other topics might be paperwork, punctuality, what respect looks like, dress, use of technology, etc.

- Have an affirmation session with staff in which affirmations must be given to someone in a different generation using this prompt: "One thing I have learned from you is _____."

- Have a discussion about the question "Why?" When working with people who are or may become upset, the question "Why?" is interpreted as a judgment that provokes a defensive reaction.

  - "Why did you get that tattoo?" This question is often not really a request for knowledge.

  - "Why did you do that?" This question is not looking for an explanation that will keep us from being upset. If you are asking someone to explain themselves, you are probably already upset.

  - Recognize that "What were you thinking?" is similar. It's not a "Why?" but it is still used judgmentally. Brainstorm better ways to ask questions that are less likely to imply judgment and provoke a reaction. Questions beginning with where, when, how, and who tend to be more information-based and less judgmental.

Activities to explore

- Body tells: Very few people experience stress and strong emotions without giving nonverbal cues. Learning to read people's nonverbals can be useful in deescalating a situation before it gets out of hand.

- Learn your own physical calming strategies, such as rubbing your eyes or scratching a specific spot on your arm. Most people have some physical way their body expresses a buildup of stress the body is trying to defuse. If you take time to learn yours, you may be able to deal with the stress before it increases, as your body will know and express stress before you are consciously aware of it. If you need help with this, consider asking a trusted friend, coworker, or family member. They will often know what your physical calming strategies are even if they didn't realize they did.

- People we see often are bound do things that bother us, some more than others. There are going to be conflicts, and we are going to react. How we react, and how we get better at regulating our reactions, is a large part of our effectiveness with others and satisfaction with ourselves. When you have an emotional reaction to a situation, consider this five-step process. These steps can be discussed and applied to deal with our reactions to others, whether coworkers or those we serve.

Step 1: React

- Accept that you had the emotional reaction that you had, even if it resulted in a negative behavior in word or deed.

- Validate your own emotions. Emotions are not good or bad. They just are. They are a message from the brain and body that something is going on and needs to be addressed.

Step 2: Retreat

- Step away from the situation, whether physically or just mentally. Quiet yourself, take some deep breaths, and integrate your brain. Use the hand model to remind yourself and give yourself a physical prompt.

- If you have time to step away physically before moving forward, it can help to write down or draw a picture of what happened.

Step 3: Reframe

- Consider that the other person may have an unintegrated, unregulated brain rather than accusing them of bad motivation or moral failure.

- Remind yourself that you know only a bit of the other person's story. You don't know what was going on inside their head or what the interaction brought up from their implicit emotional memories.

Step 4: Rethink

- If there is time, come up with two or three possible explanations for the behavior of the other person other than "what a jerk" or "that person's crazy."

- Talk yourself through a couple options for moving forward in the situation.

Step 5: Repair (re-act)

- If the opportunity is available, give yourself a do-over. Act again—re-act—and do what you can to repair the relationship with an appropriate apology and some problem solving.

Initially, these five steps will take time and intentionality. You may have to go through them each time an interaction is over. However, if applied regularly, they can become a mental process that you can use quickly within an interaction. Then they will be helpful as a part of deescalating what might otherwise become angry, unproductive interactions.

Chapter Six

Family Patterns in the Workplace

Families and parenting are emotional intergenerational systems

One of the basic human dilemmas is this: How do I live with a group of people and still keep my individual freedom? The first organizational structure in which a person experiences that dilemma is their family—whatever form that family might take. It is from family that we learn about trust, cooperation, competition, identity, roles, negotiation, integrity, and values.

Every family has emotional patterns that are intergenerational, and every family has stories that solidify its identity and ideas of what a family does. These patterns tend to repeat themselves generation after generation. This is because many of these emotional patterns are established before children are three years old, before they have vocabulary to name what has happened.

The research makes a distinction between family structure and family function. Examples of family structure include two-parent, single-parent, blended family, etc. Family function is the extent to which an individual within a family can get these needs met: material necessities, learning, self-respect, peer relationships, harmony, and stability.

People tend to parent either the way they were parented or in reaction to the way they were parented. And parenting is intergenerational—grandparents give advice, as do relatives.

Almost all families have secrets. These are issues and happenings that may not be discussed openly, acknowledged, or even recognized, yet they impact the family dynamics. Family therapist Virginia Satir identified that if a person dies young or unexpectedly, that person plays more of a role in the thinking of the family after their death than they did while they were alive. Why? Because they live on in the memory of the people who are still alive.[76]

The Karpman triangle

The Karpman triangle is made up of three roles: abuser, victim, and rescuer. Almost every family has at least one version of the Karpman triangle alive and well within it. In other words, the boundaries within families are messy, and the roles constantly change.[77]

Karpman Triangle

Rescuer

Abuser/
persecutor/
bully

Victim

We bring our family systems, emotional triggers, wounds, and bonding and attachment style to the workplace.

And so does everyone else.

The authors bring their emotional family systems into the workplace, and they choose their responses to other people's stories. And so does everyone else. The tacit emotional understandings that we got from our family—whatever our family might look like—we bring with us to the workplace.

How does this show up in the workplace? Supervisors, employees, and coworkers replicate family patterns. At the very simplest level it is this: Who is functioning in a motherly role? Who takes on a more fatherly role? Who acts like an older sibling? A younger child? Who acts like a middle child?

These quasi-familial patterns that develop organically in workplaces can both help and hinder productivity. One of the ways they can cause tension is by putting people into a Karpman triangle. Who engages in the triangle constantly? Do they usually play the role of the bully, the victim, or the rescuer first (since eventually everyone in the triangle will play all three roles)? Who refuses to take responsibility? Who creates drama? Who cuts people off by refusing to work with them, talk to them, or interact with them? Who dominates the discussion? What are their emotional triggers? What is their style of bonding and attachment?

Here is a series of questions you can answer about your own family's emotional patterns to begin to look at how they might crop up in other settings, like the workplace.

	In your family, who...?	In your workplace, who...?
Is an authority figure?		
Is a caretaker?		
Is exiled, separate, cut off?		
Is the favorite?		
Do you use to get leverage for something you want?		
Do you have a competitive relationship with?		
Do you have a cooperative relationship with?		
Do you go out of your way to help?		
Do you go out of your way to hurt?		
Is ignored or a loner?		
Carries secrets?		
Is a gossip?		
Has an addiction?		

(continued on next page)

(continued from previous page)

	In your family, who...?	In your workplace, who...?
Is manipulative, gets their way?		
Is unmotivated?		
Is difficult?		
Has a disability?		
Is loved and admired by everyone?		

What repeat patterns do you see?

What are other family patterns that are deeply embedded emotionally?

1. Birth-order family patterns—firstborn, second-born, middle child, youngest

A great deal of research has been done on the effects of birth order. One researcher in this area is Kevin Leman, author of *The New Birth Order Book: Why You Are the Way You Are*. Leman identifies several of the issues and the research around them.[78]

Here is a brief synopsis: Usually, the birth-order patterns most examined are those of oldest children, only children, middle children, and youngest children. A disproportional number of U.S. senators, presidents, and other leaders have been either an oldest child or an only child.

Firstborn and only children tend to have type A personalities: They are reliable, achievement driven, leadership ready, cautious, and conscientious, and they feel the need to be perfect and like to control and structure the environment. The research indicates that firstborn and only children receive more of the parents' time than other children. The research also shows that parents expect more from firstborn and only children.

Middle children typically have a large social group comprising many friends. They know how to please people, can be rebellious, feel like their needs and wants are ignored, and learn to negotiate with both older and younger siblings.

Youngest children, often called "the baby" of their families, tend to have experienced a more relaxed style of parenting and therefore tend to have more fun, know how to manipulate others to get what they want, and can be self-centered and outgoing.

2. Stepparenting family patterns

In her book *Surviving and Thriving in Stepfamily Relationships,* Patricia Papernow identifies that stepfamily and blended family patterns are a process, not an event.

The stages of a blended family are (1) getting started or stuck (lots of shame and blame), (2) immersion in the reality (insiders and outsiders—losses and loyalties), (3) awareness—clarity and acceptance, (4) mobilization (shared middle ground, differences are examined), (5) couple becomes a sanctuary, (6) resolution—holding on and letting go. If this occurs when the couple is older, then there is often a shift from blending to fostering subsystems.[79]

3. Scapegoating family patterns

This is when one person becomes the scapegoat, usually by being designated "the bad child," and is alienated from the family deliberately. It often occurs when the parents have a covert conflict and select a child to focus on, and then they project their dysfunction onto the child. In her book *Rejected, Shamed, and Blamed*, Rebecca Mandeville writes that "the narcissistic parent governing such a system requires that their children and spouse idolize and revere them. Children in such families are nothing more than mirrors whose sole purpose is to reflect back to the narcissistic parent their own imagined perfect and faultless image."[80]

4. Addiction family patterns

"The family typically adapts to the chemically dependent person by taking on roles that help reduce stress, deal with uncertainty, and allow the family to function within the craziness and fear created by the addict."[81]

These roles include the enabler (protects the addict from consequences, often in an attempt to control the situation), the hero (overperforms, is "too good to be true," hopes that by being "good" the addict will stop, allows emotional pain to be ignored), the scapegoat (creates problems to distract from the real issue), the lost child (ignores the problem, may become isolated), and the mascot (uses humor to escape pain and lighten the situation).[82]

According to American Addiction Centers, these are common characteristics of adult children of alcoholics:

- Being unable to trust yourself or others

- Hypervigilance in social interactions

- Feeling hypersensitive to comments from others

- Being guarded in your personal communications

- High achievement and perfectionism

- Prioritizing the needs of others above your own

- Using conflict avoidance techniques, such as withdrawing physically or emotionally

- Feeling disconnected from your feelings of anger

- Being unable to express your feelings in appropriate ways

- Strong avoidance or escapism behaviors

- A diminished capacity to deal with negative emotions in others

- All-or-nothing or black-and-white thinking, meaning you see people and circumstances as all good or all bad

- Creating crises when there aren't any

- Low self-esteem and a lack of self-worth

- High tolerance for inappropriate or poor behavior in others[83]

5. Family patterns following the untimely death of a family member

Recall that the work of Virginia Satir found that when a person dies, particularly if the death is untimely or unexpected, the person who has died plays more of a role in the thinking of the living than they did when they were alive.

When a family member or a very close friend dies, there is almost always guilt and lots of what-ifs. "What if I had done this, what if I had done that, if only I had known…" The untimely loss of family members is particularly front and center right now because of all the deaths attributed to fentanyl overdose.

Gender and sex

Johns Hopkins University states the following:

> We begin [examining the concept of gender] by separating sex from gender. Sex refers to biological and physical characteristics that are linked with being labeled male or female. Sex is labeled at birth, usually on the basis of genitalia and/or chromosomes. **Gender** refers to the combination of characteristics, expectations, and roles usually associated with biological sex—often placed on a spectrum between masculine and feminine. The concept of gender is complicated because most aspects of gender are social constructs that vary across time and culture. For example, **gender presentation** (appearance, clothing, mannerisms, and behaviors) and **gender roles** (social roles, occupational choices) vary widely depending on the culture and era.[84]

It should be noted that there are male and female genitalia and chromosomes. Between 0.5% and 1.8% of the total population is born with either no genitalia or double genitalia, which is called intersex. While everyone is familiar with XX and XY chromosomes, there are also XXY, XXXY, XYY, and X0 combinations. *The Economist* reported that around the world, since 1970, the sperm count has dropped by 50%.[85] This is because the water supply is polluted with estrogen because of all the plastics in the water and the growth hormones given to plump up animals' meat. There are more birth variations now than ever before.

Genetic research has discovered chimeras, which are "organism[s] whose cells are derived from two or more zygotes." In other words, it is possible for one human body to have two sets of DNA, and one way it can occur is when fetal cells cross the placental barrier. Sex-discordant chimerism can be a reason a person might reject the gender they were assigned at birth.[86]

Epigenetics can impact sex as well. Epigenetics is the ability of the environment to change the way your genes are expressed.

Male and female differences

The concept of gender has become a pressing issue today. Is gender determined by sex assignment at birth? Are males those with XY chromosomes and females those with XX chromosomes (nature), or is gender determined by social/cultural norms (nurture)? Researchers are constantly examining and interpreting their findings, and they don't always agree. One of the main problems with the research is that the samples are small and subject to political interpretation. If you apply the research findings to only one sex or the other, someone will always find the exception and claim the research is flawed or biased.

There are a number of patterns or tendencies that can be found that show some similarities and differences between males and females. These patterns can have a major impact on learning and people's ability to deal with emotional problems. One tendency or pattern is not better than another, nor is one right and the other wrong. There are always exceptions to these patterns, and it would be absolutely wrong to assume that these patterns are absolutes. Assuming that the patterns are absolutes is what leads to bias and stereotyping. Men and women can do the same things; they may just do them differently.

How to apply this information in your workplace

1. Is the Karpman triangle alive and well in your workplace? Who gets caught in the triangle most often?

2. What is the birth order of your boss? What is your birth order? How do your birth orders affect your interactions?

3. What family patterns do you see yourself repeating at work? Do those patterns help you or hurt you in the particular workplace you are in right now?

Journaling questions and prompts

- Reflect on the chart near the beginning of the chapter. Write about how the people you work with remind you of specific members of your family. How is your response to those coworkers reflective of your relationships with family members?

- Think of a conflict situation you experienced recently. Did you take on the roles in the Karpman triangle? Which role do you find yourself gravitating toward the most?

- For parents: In your reactions to your children, have you noticed similarities with how you were raised? Generational transfer is real! How are you using what you learned as a child, both positively and negatively, to raise your own kids?

- Write a letter to your parents (that you will likely never send) identifying both the positive and negative things you gained from them as you grew up. This letter could be used as the starting point for a conversation with a trusted friend or counselor.

Discussion questions for staff

- If your staff is safe emotionally, the discussion prompt "You remind me of my family member because _____..." could be useful in building deeper connections between staff members through sharing more of each other's stories.

- A staff discussion about gender stereotypes will help to highlight what people already know but didn't realize was true, and it will help take some of the generalizations out of the information. This can also lead to a positive discussion about differences in general and how to take advantage of differences to build a strong staff community.

Activities to explore

- Draw your family tree, including notes about everything you know about the relationships and personalities of the last three generations (or more if you're able). What was Uncle Joe like as a person? What was the relationship like between Grandpa Willie and Grandma Julie? Can you trace any significant factors throughout the generations, like involvement in a church, membership in a labor union, or the impact of alcohol and addiction?

Chapter Seven

What Can a Leader Do to Promote More Emotional Stability?

There are many strategies and practices leaders can implement at work that foster emotional stability across the organization.

1. Examine safety and belonging in your organization.

My, Ruby's, student teaching experience in a middle school was brutal. It was so stressful that I would throw up many mornings before I went to the school. My supervising teacher was callous and uncaring toward me, toward the students, and, as I later learned, toward her own children.

The way the program was supposed to work was that you were to student teach for six weeks. The first week you were supposed to do one class, the second week two classes, etc., until you were teaching a full day. That is not the way mine went.

The first week I was there, the supervising teacher said, "Okay, starting next week you will teach all day, all six classes. This is a break for me. And, by the way, I am way behind on grading," and she gave me a stack of papers to grade that was two feet high. Last, but not least, she told me that I would occasionally need to babysit her children on the weekends! I was waiting tables at the time and could make up to $100 in tips on a good night. For a 3–4 hour evening of babysitting, the supervising teacher would give me $1. But I babysat because I really wanted to teach, and I wanted a good recommendation.

2. How are weaknesses and strengths examined? How does validation occur?

I, Ruby, grew up on a farm. On the farm, in order for everyone to survive, the focus was on what people could do well. You were constantly looking to identify who could do what well. To focus on what people could *not* do well was not beneficial to productivity. Everyone had to do a part in order for the farm to survive. It was not permissible for someone to do nothing. You had to contribute. The issue was where you could contribute the most.

In my business, that is still my philosophy. I know businesses that constantly fire and hire. The problem with that is there is not internal stability. There is barely time to get to know people. Trust is limited. Turf is protected. Tacit knowledge bases are not shared.

At the time that I first heard of Jack Welch's idea of firing the bottom 10% of employees every year, rank ordering everyone, I said to a friend of mine, "That is unproductive. You spend so much time and energy rank ordering— looking at what people cannot do—that it becomes difficult to develop long-term momentum." When Jack Welch left, General Electric came apart. It has never again achieved its prior level of market share or value. And any company that has adopted that philosophy, according to a recent study, has also lost market share and value.

3. As a leader, what are the emotional family patterns you bring to the workplace?

Sally came from a family where her mother manipulated her father behind the scenes to get what she (the mother) wanted. Sally took a job, and the boss reminded her of her father. She approached the boss about doing a project but he said no, so Sally had a coworker take the idea to the boss. Again, the boss said no. Sally then arranged for a board member to take the idea to a board meeting to pressure the boss to accept it. The boss was furious that the protocols had been broken. The boss confronted Sally and told her it could not happen again.

The emotional family patterns Sally had learned at home replayed themselves at work. When she tried to manipulate her boss like her mother had manipulated her father, the strategy not only failed, but it brought her into conflict with her boss and earned her a reprimand.

Emotional wellness in the workplace determines rates of retention, productivity, and stability.

As we understand how we begin to get our understandings of emotional well-being, we can provide better structures and supports in the workplace.

Journaling questions and prompts

- In its most basic form, leadership can be defined as influence. In that sense, we are all leaders in terms of how we influence others at home, at work, and so on. That influence can be both positive or negative, and sometimes the influence is self-serving. Consider social media influencers, for example. Write about the influence you would like to have on others. How are you developing that influence?

- Write about an important leader in your life, perhaps a parent or other relative, a mentor, a teacher, or a coach. What made them a good leader in your life? What qualities are you trying to emulate based on your relationship with them?

- For people in positions of leadership: The relationships people have with the leader are vital in determining job satisfaction and performance. Write about your relationships with the people you supervise. How are you working to improve those relationships?

Discussions questions for staff

- Using the picture of the Karpman triangle, have an open discussion about getting trapped in the triangle that includes strategies for staying out of the cycle. Discuss staying out of the triangle with clients/customers and with each other.

- Discuss rituals people have for leaving their work at work at the end of the day. Focus on rituals that help leave the emotions of work at work and promote a healthy transition to home.

- As a leader, have transparent conversations both one-on-one and with the group about what you can do to better support the staff. These are courageous conversations and require a bit of vulnerability and courage, but they can be powerful in letting staff members know they are seen and heard.

Activities to explore

- In addition to being leaders in terms of influence, we are also the ultimate leaders of ourselves. To promote emotional stability, consider developing a strategy for self-care along these lines:

  I will take care of myself…

  - Spiritually, with gratitude, prayer, meditation, and nature

  - Physically, with diet, exercise, and healthy sleep habits

  - Intellectually, by reading, learning new things, and enjoying hobbies not related to work

  - Relationally, with friendships, intentional repair, and time with family

  - Emotionally, through journaling, validation of my emotions, and transparent conversations with a close friend, family member, or counselor

  A good way to get started is to pick one small thing in each area to work on or add, or maybe just one thing in one area. It is better to make small gains in taking care of yourself than to set ambitious goals that are unattainable. Failing to meet unrealistic goals perpetuates the voice of shame that says you can't, you are not enough, you will always be this way.

- There are a lot of good materials out there for understanding and improving staff dynamics. Consider doing a staff book study of Patrick Lencioni's *The Five Dysfunctions of a Team.*

Conclusion

The authors hope the insights and tools in this book will help you achieve and maintain well-being in your career and in your life outside of work. When you're experiencing stress or having trouble understanding your colleagues' behavior, revisit the research covered here and use the suggested activities and discussion questions. If we work first to understand, we'll reduce stress, improve productivity, and be happier in our careers and in our lives.

Personal Notes and Reflections

Endnotes

[1] C. M. Tyng et al., "The Influences of Emotion on Learning and Memory"

[2] D. Siegel, *Mindsight*

[3] *Ibid.,* page 18

[4] *Ibid.,* pages 18–19

[5] M. M. Kishiyama et al., "Socioeconomic Disparities Affect Prefrontal Function in Children"

[6] D. Siegel, *Mindsight,* page 26

[7] S. Stosny, *The Powerful Self*

[8] D. Siegel, *Mindsight,* page 26

[9] M. Costandi, "Pregnant 9/11 Survivors Transmitted Trauma to Their Children"

[10] K. McLean et al., "The Empirical Structure of Narrative Identity"; K. McLean, *The Coauthored Self*

[11] C. Mooney, *Theories of Attachment,* page 17

[12] J. Bowlby, *Attachment*

[13] M. D. Ainsworth & S. M. Bell, "Attachment, Exploration, and Separation"

[14] S. Stosny, *Treating Attachment Abuse,* page 21

[15] *Ibid.,* page 22

[16] *Ibid.*

[17] *Ibid.*

[18] *Ibid.,* page 61

[19] D. Siegel, *Mindsight,* page 171, emphasis added

[20] "Core Self-Evaluations"

[21] S. Stosny, *Treating Attachment Abuse,* page 18, emphasis in original

[22] S. Stosny, *Soar Above,* page 4, emphasis in original

[23] E. Erikson, *A Way of Looking at Things,* page 609

[24] E. Erikson, *Identity: Youth and Crisis,* page 97

[25] S. Scheck, "The Stages of Psychosocial Development According to Erik H. Erikson"

[26] E. Erikson, *Identity and the Life Cycle,* page 154

[27] *Ibid.*

[28] S. Scheck, "The Stages of Psychosocial Development According to Erik H. Erikson"

[29] *Ibid.*

[30] *Ibid.*

[31] *Ibid.*
[32] E. Erikson, *Identity: Youth and Crisis,* page 136
[33] "Understand Myself Personality Assessment"
[34] E. Barker, *Plays Well with Others*
[35] "Dominant Culture"
[36] M. Wisniewski, "In Puerto Rico, No Gap in Median Earnings Between Men and Women"
[37] "Racial Pay Gap in the United States"
[38] C. Thompson, *The Soul of Shame*
[39] C. Mooney, *Theories of Attachment*
[40] S. Stosny, *Treating Attachment Abuse,* page 52
[41] *Ibid.,* pages 50–51
[42] *Ibid.*
[43] E. Harrell et al., "Indicators of Workplace Violence, 2019"
[44] R. Maurer, "When Domestic Violence Comes to Work"
[45] S. Stosny, *Treating Attachment Abuse,* pages 92–93, emphasis added
[46] S. Akhtar & H. Parens, *Revenge,* location 118
[47] K. McLean, *The Coauthored Self,* page 27
[48] I. M. Cron and S. Stabile, *The Road Back to You*
[49] M. Rukeyser, "The Speed of Darkness"
[50] G. Miller, "How Our Brains Make Memories"
[51] K. McLean et al., "The Empirical Structure of Narrative Identity"
[52] K. McLean, *The Coauthored Self*
[53] *Ibid.*
[54] *Ibid.,* page 22
[55] *Ibid.,* page 6
[56] M. Martinez, *The MindBody Code*
[57] R. Solnit, *The Faraway Nearby,* page 246
[58] G. Sheehy, *Passages,* page 30
[59] *Ibid.,* page 31
[60] *Ibid.,* pages 331–332
[61] *Ibid.,* page 144
[62] *Ibid.,* page 185
[63] *Ibid.,* page 199
[64] *Ibid.,* page 197
[65] *Ibid.,* page 246
[66] *Ibid.,* page 348
[67] *Ibid.,* page 349
[68] *Ibid.,* page 358
[69] *Ibid.,* page 46
[70] *Ibid.,* page 168
[71] *Ibid.,* pages 365–366
[72] *Ibid.,* page 368
[73] Note that this is based on statistics about machinists, but similar trends exist in many professions; J. Schleckser, "If You Work with Your Mind, There's No Retirement for You"; A. Brenoff, "Early Retirement May Be the Kiss of Death, Study Finds"
[74] G. Sheehy, *Passages,* page 484
[75] M. Dimock, *Defining Generations: Where Millennials End and Generation Z Begins*
[76] V. Satir, *Peoplemaking*
[77] S. Karpman, "Fairy Tales and Script Drama Analysis"
[78] K. Leman, *The New Birth Order Book*
[79] P. Papernow, *Surviving and Thriving in Stepfamily Relations*

[80] R. Mandeville, *Rejected, Shamed, and Blamed*
[81] MARR Addiction Treatment Centers, "Roles in the Addicted Family System"
[82] *Ibid.*
[83] American Addiction Centers, "Children of Alcoholics"
[84] Johns Hopkins University, "Introduction to Transgender Identities," emphasis in original
[85] "Sperm Counts Are Falling Precipitously Across the Rich World"
[86] K. Madan, "Natural Human Chimeras"

Bibliography

Ainsworth, M. D., & Bell, S. M. (1970). Attachment, exploration, and separation: Illustrated by the behavior of one-year-olds in a strange situation. *Child Development, 41*(1), 49–67. https://doi.org/10.2307/1127388

American Addiction Centers. (2022, September 14). Children of alcoholics: The impacts of alcoholics on kids. https://americanaddictioncenters.org/alcoholism-treatment/children

Bowlby, J. (1969). *Attachment: Attachment and loss* (vol. 1). Basic Books.

Clear, J. (2018). *Atomic habits: An easy and proven way to build good habits and break bad ones.* Avery.

Cloud, H., & Townsend, J. (1992). *Boundaries: When to say yes, how to say no to take control of your life.* Zondervan. Core self-evaluations. (2022). Wikipedia. https://en.wikipedia.org/wiki/Core_self-evaluations

Costandi, M. (2011, September 9). Pregnant 9/11 survivors transmitted trauma to their children. *The Guardian.* https://www.theguardian.com/science/neurophilosophy/2011/sep/09/pregnant-911-survivors-transmitted-trauma

Cron, I. M., & Stabile, S. (2016). *The road back to you: An Enneagram journey to self-discovery.* IVP Books.

Dimock, M. (2019). Defining generations: Where Millennials end and Generation Z begins. Pew Research Center. https://www.pewresearch.org/fact-tank/2019/01/17/where-millennials-end-and-generation-z-begins/ft_19-01-17_generations_2019/

Dominant culture. (2022). Oxford Reference. https://www.oxfordreference.com/view/10.1093/oi/authority.20110803095725838

Dweck, C. S. (2006). *Mindset: The new psychology of success.* Ballantine Books.

Erikson, E. (1968). *Identity: Youth and crisis.* Norton.

Erikson, E. (1980). *Identity and the life cycle.* Norton.

Erikson, E. (1987). *A way of looking at things: Selected papers from 1930 to 1980.* Norton.

Goldman, B. (2017, Spring). Two minds: The cognitive differences between men and women. *Stanford Medicine.* https://stanmed.stanford.edu/how-mens-and-womens-brains-are-different/

Goleman, D. (1995). *Emotional intelligence: Why it can matter more than IQ.* Bantam Books.

Hanson, R. (2020). *Neurodharma: New science, ancient wisdom, and seven practices of the highest happiness.* Harmony Books.

Harrell, E., Langton, L., Petosa, J., Pegula S. M., Zak, M., Derk, S., Hartley, D., & Reichard, A. (2022, July). Indicators of workplace violence. Violence in the Workplace (series). NCJ Number 250748. U.S. Bureau of Justice Statistics. https://bjs.ojp.gov/library/publications/indicators-workplace-violence-2019

Johns Hopkins University. (n.d.) Introduction to transgender identities. https://studentaffairs.jhu.edu/lgbtq/education/intro-trans/

Karpman, S. (1968). Fairy tales and script drama analysis. *Transactional Analysis Bulletin, 7*(26), 39–43.

Kishiyama, M. M., Boyce, W. T., Jimenez, A. M., Perry, L. M., & Knight, R. T. (2009). Socioeconomic disparities affect prefrontal function in children. *Journal of Cognitive Neuroscience, 21*(6), 1106–1115. https://doi.org/10.1162/jocn.2009.21101

Leaf, C. (2021). *Cleaning up your mental mess: 5 simple, scientifically proven steps to reduce anxiety, stress, and toxic thinking.* Baker Books.

Leman, K. (1998). *The new birth order book: Why you are the way you are.* Revell.

Lencioni, P. (2002). *The five dysfunctions of a team: A leadership fable.* Jossey-Bass.

Madan, K. (2020). Natural human chimeras: A review. *European Journal of Medical Genetics, 63*(9). https://doi.org/10.1016/j.ejmg.2020.103971

Mandeville, R. C. (2020). *Rejected, shamed, and blamed: Help and hope for adults in the family scapegoat role.* Kindle Direct.

MARR Addiction Treatment Centers. (n.d.). Roles in the addicted family system. https://www.marrinc.org/roles-in-the-addicted-family-system/

Martinez, M. (2016). *The mindbody code: How to change the beliefs that limit your health, longevity, and success.* Sounds True.

Maurer, R. (2022). When domestic violence comes to work. Society for Human Resource Management. https://www.shrm.org/resourcesandtools/hr-topics/risk-management/pages/domestic-violence-workplace-nfl-ray-rice.aspx

McLean, K. C. (2016). *The coauthored self: Family stories and the construction of personal identity.* Oxford University Press.

McLean, K. C., Syed, M., Pasupathi, M., Adler, J. M., Dunlop, W. L., Drustrup, D., Fivush, R., Graci, M. E., Lilgendahl, J. P., Lodi-Smith, J., McAdams, D. P., & McCoy, T. P. (2020). The empirical structure of narrative identity: The initial big three. *Journal of Personality and Social Psychology, 119*(4), 920–944. https://doi.org/10.1037/pspp0000247

Miller, G. (2010, May). How our brains make memories. *Smithsonian Magazine.* https://www.smithsonianmag.com/science-nature/how-our-brains-make-memories-14466850

Mooney, C. G. (2009). *Theories of attachment: An introduction to Bowlby, Ainsworth, Gerber, Brazelton, Kennell, and Klaus.* Redleaf Press.

Navarro, J. (2008). *What every body is saying: An ex-FBI agent's guide to speed reading people.* HarperCollins.

Papernow, P. (2013). *Surviving and thriving in stepfamily relations: What works and what doesn't.* Routledge.

Payne, R. K. (2018). *Emotional poverty in all demographics: How to reduce anger, anxiety, and violence in the classroom.* aha! Process.

Payne, R. K. (2020). *Emotional poverty, volume 2: Safer students and less-stressed teachers.* aha! Process.

Payne, R. K., DeVol, P. E., & Dreussi-Smith, T., with Krebs, E. K. (2022). *Bridges out of poverty: Strategies for professionals and communities* (5th ed.). aha! Process.

Pink, D. H. (2009). *Drive: The surprising truth about what motivates us.* Riverhead Books.

Racial pay gap in the United States. (2022). Wikipedia. https://en.wikipedia.org/wiki/Racial_pay_gap_in_the_United_States

Rukeyser, M. (n.d.). The speed of darkness. Poetry Foundation. https://www.poetryfoundation.org/poems/56287/the-speed-of-darkness

Satir, V. (1972). *Peoplemaking.* Science and Behavior Books.

Scheck, S. (2005). The stages of psychosocial development according to Erik H. Erikson (excerpt). https://www.grin.com/document/284265

Sheehy, G. (1977). *Passages: Predictable crises of adult life.* Bantam.

Siegel, D. (2010). *Mindsight: The new science of personal transformation.* Bantam.

Solnit, R. (2013). *The faraway nearby.* Penguin.

Sperm counts are falling precipitously across the rich world. (2021, May 19). *The Economist.* https://www.economist.com/graphic-detail/2021/05/19/sperm-counts-are-falling-precipitously-across-the-rich-world

Stosny, S. (1995). *Treating attachment abuse: A compassionate approach.* Springer.

Stosny, S. (2003). *The powerful self: A workbook for therapeutic self-empowerment.* CompassionPower.

Stosny, S. (2016). *Soar above: How to use the most profound part of your brain under any kind of stress.* Health Communications.

Thompson, C. (2010). *Anatomy of the soul: Surprising connections between neuroscience and spiritual practices that can transform your life and relationships.* Tyndale House.

Thompson, C. (2015). *The soul of shame: Retelling the stories we believe about ourselves.* Intervarsity Press.

Tyng, C. M., Amin, H. U., Saad, M. N. M., & Malik, A. S. (2017). The influences of emotion on learning and memory. *Frontiers in Psychology, 8,* 1454. https://doi.org/10.3389/fpsyg.2017.01454

Understand Myself Personality Assessment. (2022). https://www.understandmyself.com/

van der Kolk, B. (2014). *The body keeps the score: Brain, mind and body in the healing of trauma.* Penguin.

van Edwards, V. (2017). *Captivate: The science of succeeding with people.* Penguin.

Wisniewski, M. (2022, March 1). In Puerto Rico, no gap in median earnings between men and women. United States Census Bureau. https://www.census.gov/library/stories/2022/03/what-is-the-gender-wage-gap-in-your-state.html

Index

[Page numbers in *italics* refer to tables or illustrations.]

A

Abuser, in family patterns, *102,* 102–103

ACEs. *See* Adverse childhood experiences

Activities to explore, 16–18
  attachment, 49–50
  body scan, 35
  body tells, 97
  box it up, 18
  calming techniques, 97
  family tree and patterns, 109
  identity and understanding self, 87
  leadership and self-care, 114
  motivation/managing emotions, 62–63
  practice breathing, 37
  reaction management, 98–99
  sensory scan, 36

Addiction, 12, 41, 45, 57

Addiction family patterns, 105–106

Adolescence
  attachment in, 42
  brain development in, 4–5, 9–14
  emotional development in, 9–14
  metacognition in, 11
  "once upon a time" stories in, 4–5, 9–14

  psychosocial development in (Erikson), *54–55*
  self-construction in, 51

"Adolescence of adulthood," *93*

Adult development, 14–16, 89–99
  activities to explore, 97–99
  age and, 89–90
  applying information in workplace, 96
  basic tasks of, *91–94,* 91–95
  challenges of, 95
  discussion questions about, 97
  generational characteristics and, 96
  journaling about, 96
  knowledge *versus* wisdom, 95
  mentoring and, 95
  "once upon a time" stories and, 5, 14–16
  psychosocial (Erikson's stages), *55, 56*
  Sheehy on, 90

Adult voice, 49

Adverse childhood experiences (ACEs), 11, 70

Affirmations, 97

Age
  emotional *versus* chronological, 57
  and stages of adult development, 89–90

S

About the Authors

Ruby K. Payne, Ph.D. is CEO and founder of aha! Process and an author, speaker, publisher, and career educator. She is a leading expert on the mindsets of economic class and on crossing socioeconomic lines in education and work. Payne is recognized internationally for her foundational and award-winning book, *A Framework for Understanding Poverty*, now in its sixth edition, which has sold more than 1.8 million copies. Payne has helped students and adults of all economic backgrounds achieve academic, professional, and personal success.

Payne's expertise stems from more than 30 years of experience in public schools. She has traveled extensively and has presented her work throughout North America and in Europe, Australia, China, and India. She has spoken to more than 2 million educators and trained more than 7,000 trainers to do her work. Her speaking engagements have included EARCOS (East Asia Regional Council of Schools) in Malaysia, National Association of School Boards, Central States Bankers Conference, Federal Reserve Board of Governors, Beijing Institute of Education, Harvard Summer Institute for Principals, as well as thousands of individual school districts and campuses.

Payne has written or coauthored more than a dozen books. Recent publications are the popular and award-winning *Emotional Poverty in All Demographics*, *Emotional Poverty, Volume 2*, the digital (and free) *Before You Quit Teaching*, which won the Independent Publisher Book Awards gold medal for an adult informational ebook, the revised edition of *Research-Based Strategies: Narrowing the Achievement Gap for Under-Resourced Students* (coauthored with Bethanie H. Tucker, Ed.D.), which won the Independent Publisher Book Awards bronze educational resource award, *How Much of Yourself Do You Own? A Process for Building Your Emotional Resources* (coauthored with Emilia O'Neill-Baker, Ph.D.), and the third revised edition of *Removing the Mask: How to Identify and Develop Giftedness in Students from Poverty* (coauthored with Paul D. Slocumb, Ed.D. and Ellen Williams, Ed.D.). The previous edition of *Removing the Mask* won a gold medal from the Independent Publisher Book Awards.

Another major publication is *Bridges Out of Poverty* (coauthored with Philip E. DeVol and Terie Dreussi-Smith), which offers strategies for building sustainable communities. Payne's mission of raising student achievement and overcoming poverty has become a cornerstone for school improvement efforts undertaken by educational districts and Bridges communities across the United States.

Other publications include *Under-Resourced Learners: 8 Strategies to Boost Student Achievement, Hidden Rules of Class at Work* (coauthored with Don Krabill), *School Improvement: 9 Systemic Processes to Raise Achievement* (coauthored with Donna Magee, Ed.D.), *Crossing the Tracks for Love: What to Do When You and Your Partner Grew Up in Different Worlds, Living on a Tightrope: A Survival Handbook for Principals* (coauthored with William Sommers, Ph.D.), *What Every Church Member Should Know About Poverty* (coauthored with Bill Ehlig), *Achievement for All: Keys to Educating Middle Grades Students in Poverty* (published by the Association for Middle Level Education), and *Boys in Poverty: A Framework for Understanding Dropout* (coauthored with Paul D. Slocumb, Ed.D. and published by Solution Tree Press), which received the Distinguished Achievement Award from the Association of Educational Publishers in the professional development category.

Payne received a bachelor's degree from Goshen College, a Master's Degree in English Literature from Western Michigan University, and her Ph.D. in Educational Leadership and Policy from Loyola University Chicago.

Jim Ott, S.Psy.S. spent 36 years as a school psychologist serving PK–12 schools in rural Eastern Iowa. Since retiring in 2018, he has worked independently as a consultant to schools, community organizations, and churches addressing issues related to poverty, mental health, and the emotional development of children. He has filled in as a school counselor, an elementary principal, and an interim pastor and was directly involved in forming a high school student council for a homeschooling network. He also does individual counseling and coaching with high school and postsecondary students.

Jim was a founder and leader in a Bridges Out of Poverty initiative in Dubuque, Iowa. Through this initiative, Jim assisted in facilitating Getting Ahead in a Just-Gettin'-By World groups for adults who have experienced poverty. During Jim's time with the initiative, more than 200 adults graduated from Getting Ahead groups.

Since 2010, Jim has served as a national consultant with aha! Process. Jim leads workshops for Bridges Out of Poverty, Getting Ahead, Emotional Poverty and Emotional Poverty 2, and A Framework for Understanding Poverty. In addition to these workshops, Jim addresses issues related to implicit bias in individuals and organizations. Jim also helps resettle Afghan refugees in the United States.

Jim lives in Dubuque, Iowa, with his wife of four decades, Teresa. They live in an 1880s brick home, which makes home repair and maintenance a necessary hobby. They have four adult children and four grandchildren, all of whom are the delights of their lives.

Connect with us at ahaprocess.com

- **Visit ahaprocess.com for free resources: articles, video clips, and success stories from practitioners—and read our aha! Moments blog!**

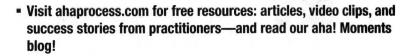

- **Sign up for our latest LIVE online workshop offerings at ahaprocess.com/events**
    - Navigating Emotional Realities with Adults
    - Bridges Out of Poverty workshop AND trainer certification
    - Workplace Stability workshop AND trainer certification
    - Getting Ahead in the Workplace certified facilitator training

- **Register for on-demand workshops at ahaprocess.com/on-demand**

- **If you like *Navigating Emotional Realities with Adults*, check out these publications:**
    - *Workplace Stability: Creating Conditions That Lead to Retention, Productivity, and Engagement in Entry-Level Workers* (Weirich)
    - *Bridges Out of Poverty: Strategies for Professionals and Communities* (Payne, DeVol, Dreussi-Smith, Krebs)
    - *Bridges Across Every Divide: Policy and Practices to Reduce Poverty and Build Communities* (DeVol, Krebs)

- **Connect with us on Facebook, Twitter, and Instagram—and watch our YouTube channel**

For a complete listing of products, please visit ahaprocess.com

Join us on Facebook
facebook.com/rubypayne
facebook.com/bridgesoutofpoverty
facebook.com/ahaprocess

Twitter
@ahaprocess
#AddressPoverty
#BridgesOutofPoverty

Subscribe to our YouTube channel
youtube.com/ahaprocess

Read our blog
ahaprocess.com/blog

Instagram
@ahaprocess